Civil War Oddities
~OF~ West Virginia

RETURN OF A FORAGING PARTY TO PHILIPPI, VIRGINIA.—[See Page 510.]

Civil War Oddities
OF West Virginia

Strange Tales of Soldiers, Civilians,
and the Supernatural

Hunter Lesser

Charleston, West Virginia

Quarrier Press
Charleston, WV

Copyright © 2022, Hunter Lesser

All rights reserved. No part of this book may be reproduced in any form or means, electronic or mechanical, including photocopying, recording, or by any information storage and retrieval system, without permission in writing from the publisher.

Book and cover design: Mark S. Phillips

ISBN-13: 978-1-942294-33-7
ISBN-10: 1-942294-33-6

10 9 8 7 6 5 4 3 2 1

Printed in the United States of America

Distributed by:

West Virginia Book Co.
1125 Central Ave.
Charleston, WV 25302
www.wvbookco.com

Table of Contents

Introduction vii

1861—A Mad Rush To Arms 1

1862—Strange Struggle for Statehood 33

1863—Raids, Refugees, and Emancipation 56

1864—Bushwackers and Land Pirates 75

1865—From Ruin to Restoration 93

An Odd Conclusion! 101

Endnotes 102

Bibliography 113

Introduction

It is strange that no book on the Civil War oddities of West Virginia has appeared, for West Virginia may be the "oddest" state in America. Severed from Virginia in the midst of the Civil War, West Virginia's strange creation echoed the issues that divided a nation. She is truly a "child of the storm."

The Mountain State is unique in so many ways. Her strange geography (not one panhandle, but two!), odd origin, and distinctive culture are all legacies of the Civil War. Although forged as a Union state, her population was bitterly divided. It should be no surprise that her Civil War stories are filled with countless oddities, weird events, and wonder.

The first campaign of the war began here—with a pledge by the Union commander to preserve slavery! A woman fired the first shot of the opening battle. West Virginians fought in armies North and South, often faced each other on the battlefield, and sometimes switched sides. Meanwhile, loyal citizens launched a Union government in Wheeling to counter the Confederate regime in Richmond. Enslaved people found freedom without the Emancipation Proclamation, as the "clash of brothers" became a struggle of sisters, spouses, and all manner of cousins.

Strangest of all, these stories are true—each one discovered by pouring through old letters, diaries, newspapers, books and journals. Soldiers and civilians are equally represented by oddities. The abolition of slavery is tethered to the very strange story of West Virginia statehood. A few well-established ghost tales have been added for spice; who's to say they didn't happen? References for each oddity can be found in the endnotes, a valuable first stop for anyone wishing to learn more. I hope these odd snippets of West Virginia's role in the Civil War will stimulate readers to dig deeper into the amazing history of the Mountain State.

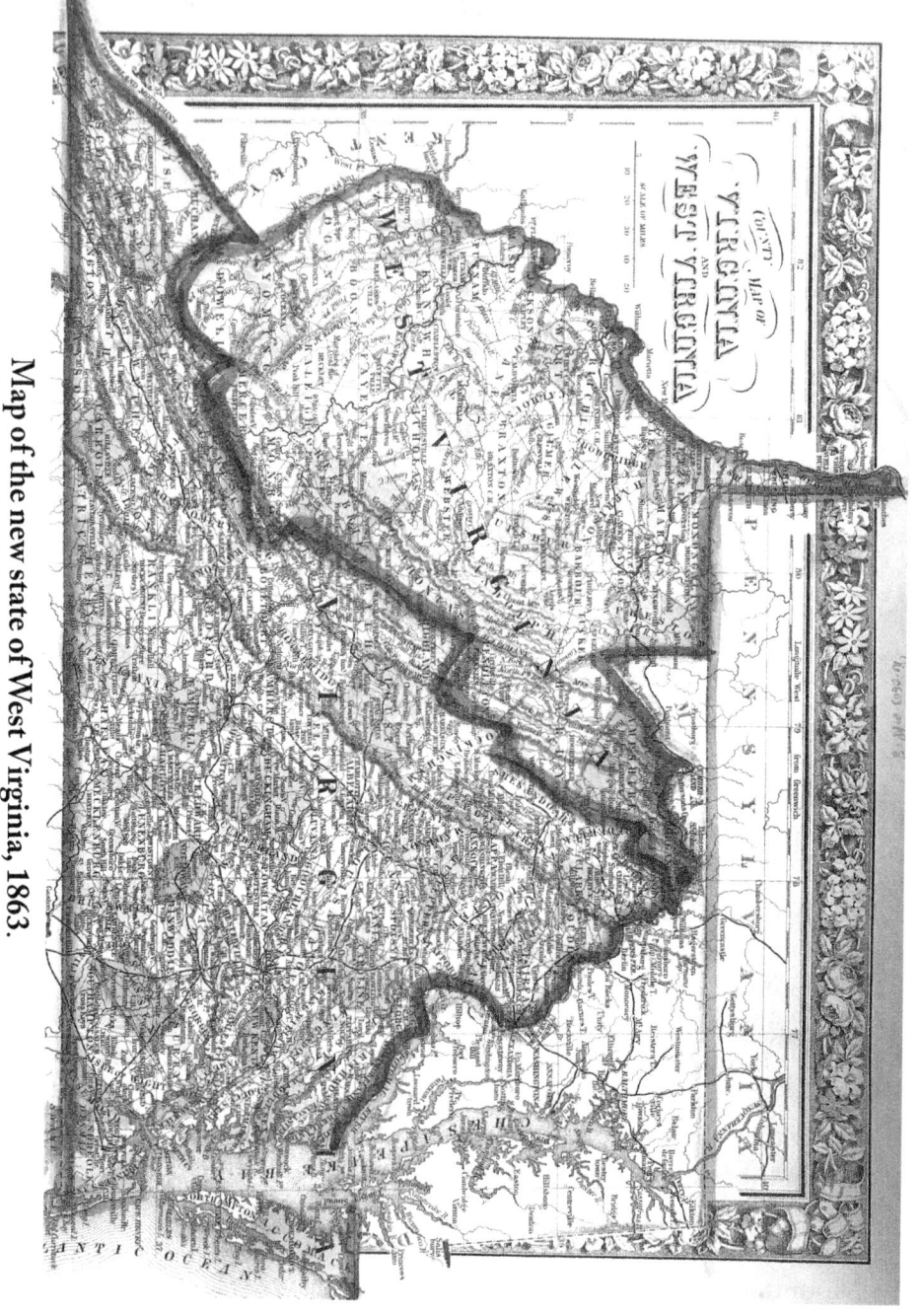

Map of the new state of West Virginia, 1863. Berkeley and Jefferson Counties were added later. (Author's collection.)

1861—A Mad Rush to Arms

Summary of Events:

"Citizen-soldiers" choose sides and rush to arms.

The first campaign of the Civil War opens in "Western" Virginia (West Virginia statehood would not be secured until 1863).

Union Gen. George McClellan becomes the North's first battlefield hero with victories at Philippi, Rich Mountain and Corricks Ford.

Virginia Unionists form a competing state government.

Gen. Robert E. Lee tries to reclaim Virginia's western counties for the Confederacy, but fails miserably in his first campaign of the war at Cheat and Sewell Mountains.

Families are caught in the crossfire.

Old rivals Henry Wise and John Floyd bicker like schoolboys as Union Gens. Jacob Cox and William Rosecrans battle them in the Kanawha Valley-New River region.

Armies clash along the Staunton-Parkersburg Turnpike, and settle into stalemate on the mountaintops for a long, punishing winter.

A House Divided!

Patriotic volunteers rallied to the call to arms in 1861. True "citizen-soldiers," they came from every walk of life. The public sentiment was sharply divided in "Western" Virginia. Loyal Unionists joined U.S. Virginia regiments, often accompanied by volunteers from neighboring northern states. Many state residents enlisted in Virginia regiments fighting for the Confederacy. A surprising number of individuals eventually fought in *both* armies![1]

Dueling Clarksburg Resolutions

On April 22, more than 1,000 Unionists gathered at a mass meeting in Clarksburg. Led by statehood firebrand John Carlile, they passed resolutions to counteract Virginia's decision to leave the Union. Strangely, just four days later, another large crowd of citizens rallied in Clarksburg for a "Southern Rights" convention in support of the Confederacy![2]

Going North or South?

The 1st (U.S.) Virginia Infantry and other "loyal" regiments mustered into service at Wheeling, a well-known hotbed of Unionism. Yet the "Shriver Grays," a Confederate company destined to serve in the Stonewall Brigade, also came from Wheeling. In Clarksburg, Union and Confederate recruits drilled at the courthouse on alternate days and locked up their weapons at night to avoid conflict. Bantering and good wishes were exchanged as they marched off to war. They would later meet in deadly earnest on the battlefield.[3]

Fearsome Monikers

The volunteers of 1861 joined companies of 75-100 soldiers (ten companies made up a regiment). These companies often took patriotic, fearsome or fanciful names. Among those campaigning in West Virginia were the Border Rangers, Iron Guards, Kanawha Riflemen, Upshur Grays, Pendleton Minutemen, New Garden Fearnots,

Greenbrier Sharp Shooters, Wise Yankee Catchers, Pocahontas Rescues, Elk River Tigers, Flat Top Copperheads and Hot Springs Hornets. And they believed it![4]

Child of the Regiment

Fourteen year-old Lucien "Cooney" Ricketts tried to enlist with the Confederate "Border Rangers" (Co. E, 8th Virginia Cavalry), led by Albert Gallatin Jenkins. When told he was too young for service, Cooney replied: "I can carry water, I can wait on you and do anything, but I am determined to go to war." Cooney was adopted as the "Child of the Regiment." He served faithfully, survived the war and became the prosecuting attorney of Cabell County.[5]

Laura Jackson Arnold—*this strong-willed sister of Confederate Gen. "Stonewall" Jackson nursed Union soldiers as fast as her brother could wound them.*
(West Virginia and Regional History Center)

Brother vs. Sister

Orphaned at an early age, Thomas Jonathan Jackson and his sister

Laura loved each other deeply. Their bond remained strong, even after they lived apart, married and had children. However, the outbreak of war ended all communication between the two. Thomas joined the Confederate army and gained fame as General "Stonewall" Jackson. Laura remained a staunch Unionist. Every bit as strong-willed and principled as her brother, Laura Jackson Arnold became a noted nurse in the town of Beverly. She pledged to "take care of the wounded Federals as fast as brother Thomas could wound them." Sadly, these siblings never got to reconcile—Stonewall died of complications from wounds suffered in 1863.[6]

Blue, Gray, and Gaudy

During the war's first year, there was no standard for uniform colors. Soldiers of both armies wore outfits of every conceivable style, ranging from the grand and gaudy to simple civilian garb. Union troops often wore gray uniforms (a common color for militia), while Confederates sometimes wore blue. As a result, casualties from friendly fire were all too frequent.[7]

Unlucky Lee

When war broke out, U.S. Col. Robert E. Lee was offered command of the Union Armies, but he declined the honor. Lee was unwilling to take up arms against Virginia, his native state. Instead, he resigned and accepted the command of Virginia's Confederate forces. Lee not only chose the losing side; Union soldiers ransacked his home and the army turned the property into a burial ground—Arlington National Cemetery.[8]

Calculating McClellan

George B. McClellan, a 34-year old West Point graduate and railroad president, was thought to be one of the top military minds in America. While traveling to Pennsylvania in expectation of an offer to command the troops of his home state, McClellan stopped in Ohio. Governor William Dennison offered the command of Ohio troops, and

McClellan accepted. As a Major General of Ohio volunteers, he built an army of 19,000 men from scratch and was promptly promoted to the same rank in United States service. Thus McClellan became the second highest-ranking officer in the U.S. Army—all without taking the field.[9]

Grant's Good Luck

While mustering Ohio forces, Maj. Gen. George McClellan nabbed a number of talented officers on their way to Washington for assignment. Oddly, one veteran West Pointer called at McClellan's headquarters to seek a staff appointment, but was rebuffed. McClellan knew the man, and likely remembered his reputation as a drinker. The scorned officer was Ulysses S. Grant! In hindsight, McClellan called the incident "Grant's Good Luck."[10]

Stonewall's Great Train Heist?

Col. Thomas (soon to be "Stonewall") Jackson, commanding Confederate troops at Harpers Ferry, complained to B&O Railroad authorities that the non-stop noise of trains running through the area disturbed his camps and must end. Fearing Jackson's wrath, railroad officials agreed to funnel all trains through Harpers Ferry between 11 a.m. and 1 p.m., making it the busiest railroad town in America. Then Jackson sprang the trap, severing the railroad at both ends, snaring 56 locomotives and 300 cars. Or so the story goes. This feat has been widely published, but its authenticity has been questioned. Although adding to Jackson's mystique, the great train heist might be a myth?[11]

A Bridge-Burner Ignites the First Campaign

On May 27, Maj. Gen. George McClellan ordered Union troops to cross the Ohio River and invade "Western" Virginia—thus launching the "First Campaign" of the Civil War. The invasion was triggered by Col. William Willey's destruction of B&O Railroad bridges near Mannington. Union troops later arrested "Bridge Burner" Willey in a sickbed. He pretended to be his half-brother Waitman Willey, a leading Unionist, until a Confederate commission and other incriminating papers were discovered![12]

*Union **Maj. General George McClellan** launched the first campaign of the Civil War with a pledge to protect slavery!*
(Author's collection)

The Union Army Pledges to Protect Slavery!

As Union forces rode the rails to Grafton, Gen. McClellan issued a proclamation to the citizens, reassuring them that private property would be protected, including their ownership of enslaved people. The proclamation read, in part:

"Virginians! ... Notwithstanding all that has been said by the traitors to induce you to believe that our advent among you will be signalized by interference with your slaves, understand one thing clearly—not only will we abstain from all such interference, but we will, on the contrary, with an iron hand, crush any attempt at insurrection on their part." No comment was forthcoming from the Lincoln administration.[13]

A Bridge Too Far

The Philippi Covered Bridge, built in 1852, was an apt symbol of a divided America. Lemuel Chenoweth of Beverly, a secessionist with sons in the Confederate army, erected the bridge superstructure while Emmett O'Brien, a strong Unionist, laid the stone abutments. The bridge became a focal point of the Battle of Philippi—the "first land battle" of the Civil War.[14]

The Philippi Races

The Battle of Philippi was a strange clash in many ways. A Union victory, it took place on June 3, 1861, Confederate President Jefferson Davis' birthday. A woman—Matilda Humphreys—fired the first shot. Virginia troops fought on both sides. As Union artillery opened fire at dawn, the surprised Confederates scampered out of town, some of them nearly naked. No one was killed in what became known as the "Philippi Races."[15]

James Hanger lost a leg to a cannon ball at Philippi and became the war's first amputee. He went on to invent an artificial limb that brought fortune and fame.
(Author's collection)

Hanger Invents a Limb

In the aftermath at Philippi, a Union surgeon, Dr. James Robison of the 16th Ohio Infantry, performed the war's first amputation. The victim, Confederate James E. Hanger of the Churchville Cavalry, had been struck in the leg by a cannonball. Hanger went on to invent an artificial limb that revolutionized the field. Today, Hanger Inc. remains one of the largest makers of prosthetics in the world.[16]

Gallows Humor

As the 7th Indiana Infantry marched in "double-quick" time toward the fight at Philippi, an officer was dismayed by their disorder. "Close up Boys!" he screamed, "Damn you, close up! If the enemy were to fire on you when you're straggling along that way, they couldn't hit a damn one of you!"[17]

Kelley Killed?

Col. Benjamin Kelley of the 1st (U.S.) Virginia Infantry was shot from a horse as he charged after the Rebels at Philippi. Carried into a nearby house, Kelley appeared to be mortally wounded. Newspaper headlines around the country announced his death. But the stalwart Kelley made a dramatic recovery, was awarded a general's star and went on to command the Department of West Virginia.[18]

A Shirttail "Skedaddle"

The word "skedaddle" may have been added to the English lexicon after soldiers and newspaper reporters first used the term to describe the comical flight of Confederates from Philippi.[19]

Two Virginia Governments

On June 11, a convention of more than 100 Virginia Unionists—irregularly elected, but emboldened by the presence of U.S. troops—met at Wheeling, more than 350 miles northwest of Richmond. Led by attorneys John Carlile and Francis Pierpont, they issued a "Declaration of Rights" and "An Ordinance for the Re-organization of the State Government." All state offices held by Rebels were declared vacant. Pierpont was appointed as the new governor. A rump legislature was formed, along with new members of Congress. By June 20, this convention approved the "Restored Government of Virginia" with the blessings of the Lincoln administration. A new Union government had been formed in Wheeling, ready to contest the Confederate government in Richmond![20]

The Great Gold Heist

To secure funding for the new Restored Government of Virginia, Governor Frank Pierpont sent John List of Wheeling to the Exchange

CSA Gen. Henry Wise fled the Kanawha Valley in 1861.
Wise claimed it was not a retreat—only a "retrograde movement."
(Author's collection)

Bank of Weston. Within its vault lay $27,000 in gold, earmarked for construction of the "Trans-Allegheny Lunatic Asylum." The 7th Ohio Infantry accompanied List to Weston, seized the gold and escorted it to Clarksburg in a hearse. It was the heaviest guarded "funeral" procession ever seen in the region.[21]

Contraband Caps

An unassuming wooden trunk, addressed to Mary Birkitt of Wheeling, was found unattended on a train. When Mary couldn't be summoned, it was pried open. Inside were lady's undergarments, some delicate lace, a pretty white dress, and then—two million percussion caps for muskets! "Ah, Mary," exclaimed the searcher, "that was a sorry dodge. No wonder you didn't answer when your name was called. Why, my dear Mary, you have here more caps than you could wear in a dozen lifetimes."[22]

Sara Lucy Bagby. This runaway was arrested by U.S. Marshals under the Fugitive Slave Act and returned to slavery. When her owner was jailed for disloyalty, Lucy found freedom once more. (Cleveland.com)

Free at Last?

Sara Lucy Bagby, an enslaved woman of Wheeling, escaped to freedom in Cleveland, Ohio. Hunted down by her owner, William Goshorn, she was arrested by U.S. Marshals as dictated by the Fugitive Slave Act. A Federal judge reluctantly returned Lucy to slavery, but she would have the last laugh. When Union troops occupied Wheeling, Goshorn was jailed for disloyalty and Lucy found freedom once more.[23]

A Night Attack

One dark and cheerless night, fearful of an imminent attack, the Union picket guards fortified with applejack before taking their post at a bridge near Clarksburg. Nervous hours later, they heard the distinct tread of approaching soldiers. "Halt!" cried a picket, but no answer came. The foe drew closer; the glare of bayonets could be seen. The pickets discharged their guns and fled in perfect terror. Sometime later, a brave soldier crept forward to investigate and discovered a cow in the last agonies of death, its horns gleaming in the moonlight.[24]

Memorable July Fourth

As Union brigades gathered in Buckhannon, Maj. Gen. George McClellan reviewed the "Army of Occupation" in a spectacular Independence Day parade. At noon, cannons boomed a national salute, banners waved, bugles blared, and cavalry pranced in splendor. Thousands of Union soldiers marched on parade to the music of regimental bands. Citizens came from miles around to witness the grand spectacle. "Lordy!" exclaimed a backwoods mountaineer; "I didn't know there was so many folkes in the world."[25]

A Recalcitrant Rebel

An old woman confronted Union soldiers along the road to Rich Mountain. Indignant and poor as a church mouse, she boasted that she came from a "higher sphere than they," and would "not lay down with dogs." A search of her house revealed several rifles, ammunition, and a secession flag. The flag had been made from the tail of an old shirt. The initials "J.D." and "S.C." on it, she proudly told the soldiers, stood for Jeff Davis and the Southern Confederacy.[26]

Taking Yankee Scalps!

From a letter found by Union troops on the Kanawha River: "Mat, if there is any engagement, I want you to … break my little trunk open, and take out my Bible and prayer-book, and those Boone County bonds, and save them for me. I have not read my Bible in sixteen years, but I want them saved ... *The enemy is coming up both sides of the river in a damned strong force. The orders are to scalp all we get near to.* —Capt. J. W. McSherry, Boone Rangers."[27]

Inspiring Speech?

Huddled around campfires the night before the Battle of Rich Mountain, soldiers of the 3rd Ohio Infantry pondered their fate. Imagine the funereal scene as their colonel gave this speech: "*Soldiers of the Third: The assault on the enemy's works will be made in the early morning. The Third will lead the column. The secessionists have ten thousand men and forty rifled cannon. They are strongly fortified. ... They will cut us to pieces. Marching to attack such an enemy, so entrenched and so armed, is marching to a butcher shop rather than to a battle. There is bloody work ahead. Many of you, boys, will go out who will never come back again.*" Surrounded by scores of pallid faces, a soldier recalled: "We all wanted to go home."[28]

Communist August Willich, drillmaster of the 9th Ohio Volunteer Infantry, a regiment of German Socialists. (Author's collection)

Socialists for the Union

The 9th Ohio Infantry, a regiment of German immigrants from Cincinnati's "Over the Rhine" district, was one of the best-drilled outfits in the Union army. As Maj. Gen. McClellan's pet regiment, they were the vanguard of the Union army at Rich Mountain. Many had fought in the European Revolutions of 1848, and were card-carrying Socialists. Their drillmaster, August Willich, was a radical Communist who had once challenged Karl Marx to a duel. He hoped to see slavery *and* Democracy "crushed in a common grave."[29]

A Pen Mightier Than the Sword

The Union victory at Rich Mountain (July 11) propelled George McClellan to the national stage, yet the young major general's performance there was less than stellar. First, he tried to call off the attack while a flank march by Gen. William Rosecrans was underway. McClellan failed to support Rosecrans when the battle commenced, and then wrote him off as defeated. Notified of "his" victory the next morning, McClellan sent thrilling telegrams to Washington that sparked a sensation, making him the North's first battlefield hero—a "Young Napoleon."[30]

The "Centre Shot"

At Rich Mountain, a squad of Indiana sharpshooters picked off the Confederate artillerists at will. Their success drew the fire of a squad of Rebels on the opposite mountainside. Redirecting their fire to this new threat, the Hoosiers were dismayed when their volley had no effect. Taunting their poor marksmanship, one of the Rebels turned around, dropped his drawers and offered "a glaring insult" of flesh. An outraged Hoosier replied with a "centre shot" from his Enfield rifle, leaving the poor Rebel in a rather undignified pose![31]

Cursed at Rich Mountain

John Hughes, a delegate to the Richmond "Secession" convention from Randolph County, had been a Unionist, but changed his loyalty and voted Virginia out of the Union. Angry Union delegates promptly placed a curse upon his head. Three months later, while scouting for Confederates during the Battle of Rich Mountain, Hughes mistook Rebel soldiers for the enemy, yelled "Hurrah for Lincoln," and was killed by a hail of bullets. He was the only civilian to die in the battle.[32]

Unsung Patriot

Twenty-two year old David Hart lived on a farm at the crest of Rich Mountain. A strong Unionist, he was descended from a signer of the Declaration of Independence. Brought to headquarters by Gens.

Rosecrans and McClellan, Hart guided Union forces to victory at Rich Mountain. He received no credit, but his farm was wrecked by battle and a price put on his head. Returning to Indiana with one of the Hoosier regiments, he enlisted in the Union army and gave his life a year later near Nashville, Tennessee.[33]

Dug Their Own Graves

Prior to the Rich Mountain battle, Confederates at the Hart farm dug a trench and marked it with a sign that read: "For Union Men." In a strange twist of fate, that trench was used to bury dead *Confederate* soldiers after the battle. The bodies were later disinterred and placed in a mass grave overlooking Beverly.[34]

No Provision for Prisoners

Lt. Col. John Pegram surrendered almost 600 Confederates to Gen. McClellan in Beverly after the Battle of Rich Mountain. McClellan was perplexed—no guidelines had been established for prisoners of war. Union authorities directed the prisoners to sign a "parole of honor" pledging not to take up arms, and then sent them home. However, Col. Pegram had failed to resign from the U.S. army before joining the Confederacy, and so was jailed at Fort McHenry in Baltimore.[35]

Hampden-Sydney Boys

The Confederate prisoners at Rich Mountain included a company of students from Hampden-Sydney College, led by their president, Rev. Dr. John Atkinson. Taken aghast by their tender ages, Union Gen. McClellan sent the young men home to their mothers. "Boys," he lectured them in a fatherly tone, "secession is dead in this region—go back to your college; Take your books and *become wise men.*"[36]

The Rich Mountain Ghost

Following the Battle of Rich Mountain, the Hart house served as a hospital for the wounded of both armies. Bloodstains on the floor could still be seen many years later. Some claimed the house was haunted. The ghostly apparition of soldiers appeared to residents and visitors, often moving from room to room, as if tending to the dead and wounded.[37]

Big Guns at Laurel Hill

During a sharp skirmish at Laurel Hill, near Belington, a Confederate drummer boy panicked and bolted to the rear. Halted by a stern Rebel officer waving a revolver in his face, the youth pointed to the Union artillery and exclaimed; "Hell, Lieutenant, there are bigger guns down there than that!" He kept on running.[38]

Lost in the Wilderness

Nearly four hundred members of the 1st Georgia Infantry were cut off during the Confederate retreat from Laurel Hill, and became lost in a "perfect wilderness." Stymied by immense laurel thickets, the frazzled Georgians hacked their way through with Bowie knives. Starving, they peeled and ate the bark of birch trees. Finally, after a four-day ordeal, they encountered a trapper who led them to settlements along Dry Fork. The rugged land they traversed is now the Otter Creek Wilderness.[39]

First General Falls at Corricks Ford

Confederate Gen. Robert S. Garnett was shot and killed while posting skirmishers at Corricks Ford, a river crossing on Shavers Fork in present-day Parsons. He was the first general killed during the Civil War. Garnett fell strangely, in the rear of his fleeing army, and some claimed he welcomed death rather than dishonor. A Union staff officer, Maj. John Love, discovered Garnett's body near the riverbank. It was a painful reunion, for the two men had been West Point roommates.[40]

General Garnett's Dog

Union soldiers related that a dog belonging to Gen. Garnett was on the battlefield when he was killed. During the months that followed, an Ohio infantryman claimed he saw no less than fifty dogs, each said, positively, to be the identical one belonging to the Rebel general.[41]

The Fighting Parson

One of the Indiana regiments in the fight at Corricks Ford contained a Methodist preacher, said to be one of the best shots in the regiment. He fired carefully, always with perfect coolness and a steady aim. His comrades declared that every time, after firing, he added: "And may the Lord have mercy on your soul!"[42]

Newshawks Go to War

During the First Campaign, crack journalists such as Whitelaw Reid (*Cincinnati Gazette*), William Bickham (*Cincinnati Commercial*), and Henri Lovie (*Frank Leslie's Illustrated*) traveled with the Union troops. Lovie dodged bullets on several occasions. George Buell of the *Cincinnati Times* bore dispatches to the front, rode on the skirmish line, and even grabbed a musket and charged with the 7th Indiana Infantry at Corricks Ford.[43]

Well-Equipped Rebels

Gen. Garnett's Confederate army abandoned vast quantities of equipment to hasten their retreat from Laurel Hill. Union soldiers noted that the Rebel tents and blankets were of the finest material; cots, litters, bandages and surgeons' stores were in abundance. It was in sharp contrast to the meager Union tents, the coarse blankets, the scanty supply of utensils, the lack of litters and bandages. The contrast was significant and painful.[44]

The Romance of Campaigning

As armies battled at Rich Mountain, a force of 3,000 Union troops under Gen. Jacob Cox advanced up the Kanawha River toward Charleston on stern-wheel steamboats. Bands struck up patriotic tunes as each bend in the river opened a grand new vista. Cox, perched atop the pilot boat, called it "the very romance of campaigning." But the romance was short-lived; on July 17, Confederates under Gen. Henry Wise battled Cox to a standoff at Scary Creek. In the confusion, four high-ranking Union officers fell into enemy hands.[45]

Feuding at Scary Creek

The Sandy Rangers, a cavalry company from Wayne County, were in the Confederate ranks at the Battle of Scary Creek. Known as the "Blood Tubs" for their red flannel hunting shirts and caps, they entered the fight singing a ballad: "Bullets and Steel." Reputed to be among their numbers was "Devil" Anse Hatfield, later to become famous in the Hatfield and McCoy feud.[46]

The Generals Patton

George Smith Patton of Charleston, great-grandson of Gen. Hugh Mercer of Revolutionary War fame, led the Kanawha Riflemen into battle at Scary Creek and was severely wounded. He went on to command the 22nd Virginia Infantry in many battles. Col. Patton was wounded again at Winchester in 1864 and died before receiving his promotion to general. Three of his brothers served as Confederate colonels. His grandson, Lt. Gen. George Smith Patton Jr., won fame as "Old Blood and Guts" in World War II. Maj. Gen. George Smith Patton IV served in Korea and Vietnam.[47]

Wise Meets His Match

Confederate Gen. Henry Wise, the irascible ex-governor of Virginia, attempted to claim the Littlepage Stone Mansion as his headquarters while in Charleston. Rebecca Littlepage, owner of the home, flatly refused. Outraged, Wise threatened to blow the house to bits with artillery. Rebecca defiantly stood her ground, and the red-faced general withdrew to the safety of his tent. He never occupied the mansion.[48]

A "Retrograde Movement"

Overwhelmed by enemy troops in late July, Confederate Gen. Henry Wise abandoned the Kanawha Valley, burning bridges as he fled east toward Lewisburg. Only the noncombustible stone cliffs at Hawks Nest were spared his torch. Wise claimed the Kanawha Valley was "wholly disaffected and traitorous … I have fallen back not a minute too soon." Wise insisted it was not a retreat—only a "retrograde movement."[49]

Devil Bill Parsons, the Bushwhacker.

"Devil Bill" Parsons. Cunning and "ferocious as a hyena," this dreaded bushwacker reputedly had eleven wives, one of whom was his own daughter! (Nine Months in the Quartermaster's Department)

Bushwackers in the Laurel

While the armies battled, a guerrilla war erupted. Angered by army depredations, citizens waged war against the troops, often targeting Union soldiers. Some of these "bushwackers" gained mythical status. "Devil Bill" Parsons, "ferocious as a hyena," earned a reputation for murder and mayhem. Described as a man of very "low instincts," it was said that he had eleven wives, one of whom was his own daughter![50]

CAMP ON CHEAT MOUNTAIN SUMMIT.

Cheat Summit Fort, an "impregnable" Union stronghold. Snow fell here in August 1861 as Robert E. Lee suffered his first defeat of the war. (History of the Fifth West Virginia Cavalry)

Wicked Weather on Cheat

The weather on Cheat Mountain is legendary. It should have been a warning to Union soldiers erecting a fortress there in the summer of 1861. Six years earlier, the Trotter brothers held a contract to carry mail over the mountain from Staunton to Huttonsville, a distance of more than ninety miles. But a severe winter snowstorm halted delivery. Complaints about the brothers sparked a terse reply to the postmaster general: "*Sir; If you knock the gable end out of Hell and back it up against Cheat Mountain and rain fire and brimstone on it for forty days and forty nights, it won't melt the snow enough to get your d_____ mail through on time.*"[51]

Distant Din of Battle

On the afternoon of July 21st, Confederate outposts on the crest of the Alleghenies reported strange sounds emanating from the East. Puzzled pickets listened for hours to the faint protracted "rumble." A veteran officer was finally summoned who recognized that noise. It was the muffled din of cannon fire—more than one hundred twenty miles distant as the crow flies—at the great Battle of Manassas.[52]

Cheated on the Mountaintop

Union soldiers delighted in their new camp on the summit of Cheat Mountain. "To one who loves the wildly picturesque in nature," wrote an Indiana volunteer, "this region could not fail to awe, to please, to fascinate." But the bluebird skies of July turned to cold, chiseling rains in August. Frigid winds howled through the spruces and fog shrouded the mountaintop. Tents and uniforms mildewed and fell to pieces. Frost blanketed the ground, and ice froze in buckets. On August 13, shivering soldiers were astonished as snow fell from the sky![53]

A Tennessee Hog Pen

The weather at Robert E. Lee's camps on Valley Mountain was little better than on Cheat. One Confederate insisted that it rained *32 days* that August. The roads and camps looked like a "Tennessee hog pen," mired in bottomless mud. A Confederate saw dead mules lying in the muddy road "with nothing but their ears showing." Epidemics of measles and typhoid fever swept through the camps. Soldiers sickened and died in droves. General Lee lamented that the sick list at Valley Mountain alone "would form an army."[54]

Courting the Maid of the Mist

The family of Mathias (Matthew) White lived on a hardscrabble farmstead atop Cheat Mountain. Union soldiers described the patriarch as "a gaunt, lean, half starved devil" who had never seen the inside of a schoolhouse or heard a sermon. His piety was said to consist of "playing *jigs* and *hoe downs* on an old fiddle" and "shooting mountain hawks on Sunday." A pert young woman in the house drew more approval. Known as the "Maid of the Mist," soldiers tried to court her, but she made clear that bestowal of her heart and hand should only be in exchange for "Linken's Skaalp."[55]

Saddened for his Sweetheart

John D. H. Ross of the 52nd Virginia Infantry was worried about his girlfriend back home. He did not doubt her fidelity; the problem as he saw it was this: "If I get killed, my sweetheart will miss having such a good husband. And I like the girl, I would not be willing to subject her to this great, and in these war times, irreplaceable loss."[56]

Dancing with the Devil

When a telegraph line was extended to the Union camp on Cheat Mountain, a rustic mountaineer took keen interest in the new-fangled device. He figured that a paper message could be strung along the wire, but was puzzled how it got past each pole without being torn to shreds? When the telegraph operator sent a query to Huttonsville and received an answer in fifteen minutes, the mountaineer was dumbfounded. He looked upon the contraption as witchcraft, and the operator as one who colluded with the devil.[57]

Elite Encampment

The Union camp at Elkwater was filled with young men who would go on to become leading lights of society. The rows of canvas tents in that pastoral encampment on the Tygart Valley River were thronged with future doctors, lawyers, legislators and members of Congress. Among the distinguished figures in that camp were future U.S. Senator and Supreme Court justice Stanley Matthews, and a pair of U.S. Presidents—William McKinley and Rutherford B. Hayes.[58]

Women at War

Women were active patriots, supporting the armies in myriad ways. Not all remained at home. Some joined the armies surreptitiously dressed as men. Others, like Betsy Sullivan, simply followed their husbands to war. Betsy campaigned with the 1st Tennessee Infantry at Cheat Mountain. She cared for sick and wounded soldiers, cooked, washed and darned for the regiment. Idolized by the troops as "Mother

Sullivan," she marched with a knapsack on her back and slept on the frozen ground with only a blanket, just like the men.[59]

Mishaps and Tragedy

Accidents were common in the army camps. Soldiers were struck by lightning, bitten by rattlesnakes, crushed by falling trees, and killed or mangled by knives, axes and the accidental discharge of firearms. At Camp Elkwater, a ricocheted bullet (meant for a snake) killed one soldier along the riverbank. Another thoughtlessly tossed an artillery shell into a campfire, killing and maiming several comrades. A surprising number of men were shot to death by nervous sentinels of their own commands![60]

The Sporting Life

In off-hours, soldiers dabbled at hunting and fishing. Streams filled with brook trout added variety to army rations. Deer, wild turkey and other game were pursued with mixed success. Union veteran Ambrose Bierce confessed they "were the original game-preservers of the Cheat Mountain region." Among their feats: a large black bear, caught in a log trap on that mountain, was carted to the railroad at Grafton and shipped alive to Wheeling for public display.[61]

Tarheel Moonshiners

The 16th North Carolina Infantry contained a company of moonshiners. Their camp at Huntersville was one of the finest of the war, located in a sugar maple grove on a clear mountain stream fringed with spearmint. Their captain pointed to the stream and exclaimed: "Here is the water, here is the mint; if anyone can furnish the sugar and some one the spirits, we'll have the best mint julep you ever tasted." The ingredients were secured and the boys enjoyed their "jolly, jolly grog," hidden in a fence corner to avoid the colonel, a strict disciplinarian.[62]

A Lecherous Rebel Yell

As a Tennessee brigade marched across Mingo Flats, they passed a log cabin along the roadside. At the doorway stood a "comely Virginia lass," sleeves rolled above her elbows as she eyed the approaching column. The boys hadn't seen a young woman in many weeks. When the 1st Tennessee Infantry passed, they gave that girl an ear-splitting yell that echoed from the mountainsides. Each regiment in passing picked up the cheer. The poor young lady was much embarrassed by the demonstration in her honor.[63]

Pesky Pickets

Gen. Robert E. Lee did his own reconnaissance while campaigning at Cheat Mountain. One day near a Confederate outpost, curious soldiers crowded around Lee as he examined the ground with a field glass. He turned mildly on one and ordered him to take the position of a soldier. "Forward march," Lee commanded. "By the right flank, march." When the soldier was pointed toward camp, Lee added; "Double-quick, march!" He was pestered no more. Another time, while scouting between the lines, Lee was captured by his own pickets, who assumed he was the enemy.[64]

Shorn of Their Rank

Confederate Sam Watkins recalled the scene after a sharp skirmish on Cheat Mountain. His officers had torn off all their lace and insignia of rank, fearing it would make them a target for the Yankees. "You see this was our first battle," Watkins wrote, "and the officers had not found out that minnie as well as cannon balls were blind; that they had no eyes and could not see. They thought that the balls would hunt for them and not hurt the privates. I always shot at privates. It was they that did the shooting and killing, and if I could kill or wound a private, why, my chances were so much the better."[65]

A Mystical Guide

Gen. Daniel Donelson's Confederate brigade had a long and difficult march to get in position for the attack on Cheat Mountain. Their guide, a little mountaineer named Samuel, wore a huge bee-gum hat. The soldiers thought he had crawled out from a dark cavern, and was a "second cousin to the ground squirrel family." He led the brigade up and down frightful precipices, bobbing along like a crippled ghost. It was said that Samuel induced the horses into a slumber and took them apart, carried the pieces over impassible cliffs, and then reassembled them with the command "Horses come forth." No one in the army had a better explanation.[66]

Lee's Near Misses

Gen. Robert E. Lee dodged fate several times during his failed assault at Cheat Mountain. First, the general stumbled into Union cavalry on Becky Creek and was nearly captured. Next, Confederate pickets almost shot him by mistake. Finally, a shell landed at Lee's feet near Elkwater, but miraculously failed to explode.[67]

Washington's War Trophies

Lt. Col. John Augustine Washington of Mt. Vernon, great-grandnephew of the first president and Gen. Lee's *aide-de-camp*, was killed near Elkwater on Friday the 13th of September. Washington was scouting with the general's son Rooney, who fled on the fallen officer's horse. Union authorities, intrigued by Washington's pedigree, doled out his effects as war trophies. A revolver went to the Secretary of War, another to the Indiana soldier credited with the killing. Washington's field glass, gauntlets, spurs, powder flask, large knife, letters and other objects were duly distributed. There seemed to be general disappointment that Washington's sword had escaped with his horse![68]

Battle of Knives and Forks

The 7th Ohio Infantry, led by Col. Erastus Tyler, was encamped at Kesslers Cross Lanes near Carnifex Ferry. Tyler, an old Virginia fur trader, boasted that he had returned to deal in "rebel skins." He nearly lost his own hide instead. On the morning of August 26, Confederates under Gen. John Floyd surprised Tyler's regiment at breakfast and drove them from the field. Upon learning of Floyd's victory, his old political foe, Confederate Gen. Henry Wise, jealously dismissed his rival's success as that "little battle of knives and forks at Cross Lanes."[69]

A Death Wish

Union Col. John Lowe, wrongly blamed for cowardice at Scary Creek, desperately sought redemption. His chance came on September 10th at the Battle of Carnifex Ferry. Leading his 12th Ohio Infantry regiment into the hottest of the fight, Lowe raised his sword and cried, "Follow me, my men! Charge!" He was promptly shot and killed. In conversations with comrades and letters home, Lowe had expressed a desire to die in battle.[70]

Conundrum at Carnifex Ferry

One of the oddities at the Battle of Carnifex Ferry was that both sides claimed victory. Union forces under Gen. William Rosecrans ultimately won the ground, but suffered costly casualties. Gen. John Floyd held back an overwhelming Union force that afternoon without the death of a single Confederate. Floyd's army stole away in the dead of night, crossed the rugged Gauley River canyon and escaped without detection to fight another day.[71]

The Feuding Generals

Confederate generals Henry Wise and John Floyd, both former governors of Virginia and ancient rivals, quarreled incessantly along the James River and Kanawha Turnpike as Union forces threatened them with annihilation. Unwilling to acknowledge Floyd's superior rank, Gen. Wise withheld cooperation of any kind. Exasperated by their feud, President Jefferson Davis ordered Wise back to Richmond. Summoned to the President's office, Wise remained defiant. "General Wise, I think I will have to shoot you," said the President, not entirely in jest. "Mr. President, shoot me," Wise replied. "That is all right, but for God's sake let me see you hang that damned rascal Floyd first."[72]

*Confederate **Generals Henry Wise** and **John Floyd**. These old political rivals feuded while Union forces threatened them with annihilation.* (Author's collection)

Smitten with a Stallion

On the crest of Sewell Mountain, Gen. Robert E. Lee was enamored with a handsome thoroughbred owned by Confederate Maj. Thomas Broun of the Wise Legion. Lee claimed he would need that horse, and referred to him as "my colt." When Lee departed for South Carolina, Broun's regiment was ordered to follow. Lee subsequently purchased the horse for $200 (more than $5,000 today). Named for his spirited gait, "Traveller" became Lee's legendary warhorse. Traveller's remains are buried outside of Lee's crypt in Lexington, Virginia, but his ghost is said to haunt the general's old camp on Sewell Mountain.[73]

Sleeping with the General

Gen. Lee's youthful aide Walter Taylor recalled a very cold fall night on the summit of Sewell Mountain. As the two Confederates huddled around a campfire, Lee suggested they should put their blankets together to make one bed, in order to sleep more comfortably. And so it was "vouchsafed to me to occupy very close relations with my old commander," Taylor recalled, "and to be able to testify to his self-denial … in those days of trial."[74]

Granny Lee

Robert E. Lee's campaign in West Virginia—his first of the war—ended in failure and almost wrecked his military reputation. Critics claimed Lee was "overrated," had been "clearly outgeneraled," and was "too tender of blood." Newspaper editorials mocked him as "the Great Entrencher" and "Granny Lee." Adding injury to the insults, Unionists approved an ordinance to create the new state of West Virginia before Lee left the region.[75]

Bruin or Bluff?

The cook for some Indiana officers bragged that he had killed a young bear near Camp Elkwater and would serve it for dinner the next day. By all accounts, the officers enjoyed a splendid feast. But someone noted later that a huge black curly-haired mastiff that belonged in camp had come up missing, raising doubt in the minds of many as to just what had been served![76]

Ben Summit's Flight to Freedom

Sent on an errand at Confederate Camp Bartow, an enslaved Arkansas man seized the chance to run away from his owner. "Ben" fled through the wilderness and sought asylum at the Union fortress on Cheat Mountain Summit. He was in luck—the commander there, Gen. Robert Milroy, was a staunch abolitionist. Milroy gave Ben a job at headquarters and the surname "Summit," for the place where he gained freedom. Later that fall, Ben went to Indiana to live with the general's wife and children, who offered work and taught him to read and write. He later joined the Union army and fought proudly for the freedom of his race.[77]

A Chilling Prophecy

Andrew Yeager, owner of "Travellers Repose," an idyllic inn and farmstead on the upper Greenbrier River, astonished visitors with a prediction early in 1861. Armies would contend for that secluded valley, Yeager said, "houses and barns would be put to the torch and families turned out of their homes." It all seemed unthinkable to his cheerful patrons. But Yeager's prophecy was sadly fulfilled. A few months later, armies clashed on the farmstead and riddled his home with artillery fire. Travellers Repose was put to the torch, the farm destroyed and the family driven away. Andrew and a son died of "camp fever" as refugees.[78]

Had His Name on It

The Battle of Greenbrier River (October 3) was filled with oddities. Artillery shells rained death and destruction around Confederate Camp Bartow and Travellers Repose. One shell bent a soldier's musket into the shape of a hoop. Another struck the shoulder of a Union soldier, who coolly picked up his severed arm and carried it to the rear. Ambrose Bierce recalled the death of a comrade, James Abbott of the 9th Indiana Infantry. Abbott had been struck in the side by a cannonball. "It was a solid round-shot," Bierce noted, manufactured in a private foundry, who's proprietor "had put his 'imprint' upon it: it bore, in slightly sunken letters, the name 'Abbott.'"[79]

A Fearless Feline

As Confederates cowered in their trenches during the artillery bombardment at Greenbrier River, a small kitten scurried back and forth on the parapet, oblivious to the storm of death. Whenever a cannonball kicked up the dirt nearby, the little feline pounced upon it in playful glee.[80]

Unready to Surrender

At one point during the Battle of Greenbrier River, a white flag appeared over Camp Bartow. Lacking a yellow flag to mark the hospital, a harried Confederate surgeon had unfurled it instead. When a Union messenger rode forward to inquire if the Rebels meant to surrender, Colonel Ed Johnson dismissed him with the curt reply: "go back and shoot your damn guns."[81]

The Banner Regiment

Members of the 1st Georgia Infantry proudly presented a large United States flag to their commander after the Battle of Greenbrier River. But that beautiful silk banner was not captured during the fight. It was found resting against a tree—much to the mortification of the flag bearer of the 7th Indiana Infantry, who had left it there. The Seventh would redeem themselves on other battlefields, but this embarrassing incident gave them a nickname—the "Banner Regiment."[82]

Battle of the Ballots

On November 6, just twelve days after Unionists ratified an ordinance to create the new state of West Virginia, Rebel soldiers within her borders voted in elections for the Confederacy. President Jefferson Davis and Vice President Alexander Stephens ran unopposed. Victor Vallette of the 1st Tennessee Infantry recalled: "I voted this ticket at the age of 15 years in the Confederate Army with Gen. Robert E. Lee [at present-day Marlinton]. When challenged due to my age, I replied, 'If I'm too young to vote I'm too young to fight.' I voted."[83]

Three Little Confederates

Three young boys, the oldest barely fourteen years of age, went squirrel hunting one day near Green Bank. Imagine their excitement upon finding a napping Union scout. Despite the scout's desperate pleading, the little boys leveled their squirrel rifles and made him a prisoner. Gleefully, they turned him over to the Confederate authorities at Camp Bartow, while the garrison cheered them as heroes.[84]

Defiant at Guyandotte

The Guyandotte "Massacre," a lightning raid by Confederate cavalry on November 10, routed, killed or captured some 150 Union recruits in that Ohio River village (present-day Huntington). In retaliation, Union troops burned much of the town, targeting the homes of Confederate sympathizers, of which there were a surprising number. When ordered to vacate her home, Mary Carroll barricaded her family inside and refused to leave. Frustrated bluecoats burned her barn instead, unaware that Union supplies were stored inside. Mary had the last laugh![85]

"General Drunk"

Contrary to regulations, whiskey ran rife in the army camps. Merchants smuggled liquor in harmless looking boxes of "Palm Soap." Local citizens hawked potent moonshine to the troops. Drunkenness sparked fights, insubordination and worse. "The boys are on a general drunk today & the guardhouse is full," noted a bemused soldier. A homesick Virginian wondered what his family would think if they could "see me with my large vial filled with whiskey! Not to save the life of Gen. Loring, and all the sons of bitches in the Confederate Army would I volunteer again!"[86]

A Snowball Battlefield

The first heavy snowfall in the mountains triggered great excitement among Confederates from the Deep South who had rarely seen snow. Led by their officers, the 1st and 12th Georgia Infantry regiments clashed in mock battle at Camp Bartow. Heavy volleys of icy missiles rained down on the troops. The battle lines ebbed and flowed with charges and counter-charges. The engagement closed without a decisive victory for either side and resulted in numerous casualties.[87]

Night Clothes and a War Club

During the Battle of Allegheny Mountain on Friday the 13th of

December, Col. Ed Johnson rushed into the fray in his nightclothes and slippers. Too hurried to strap on his sword, Johnson grabbed a wooden club and led the charges that won a hard-fought Confederate victory. Johnson's clothes were riddled with bullets; his war club was placed on display at the Virginia State Library, and he earned a general's star for his heroics. He also earned the nicknames "Allegheny" and "Old Clubby."[88]

Deceiving Deserters

Union Gen. Robert Milroy launched the attack at Allegheny Mountain based on claims from five Confederate deserters that their comrades were demoralized and "ready to surrender." So confident were Union troops of victory that the artillerists marched to battle without cannons, confident they could work the Rebel guns. But a deserter from Milroy's camp alerted the Confederates, who were ready for a fight. By all accounts, this was one of the fiercest battles of 1861.[89]

A Bizarre Bullet

After the fight on Allegheny Mountain, an Ohio infantryman took apart his damaged musket. Deep inside the barrel he found a pointed minié ball, nose down, on top of a round ball he had fired during the fight. It was evident that an enemy ball had entered his gun barrel at the moment of discharge. Although bullets were sometimes known to meet in midair, this was an act of singular rarity.[90]

Eating the Dead

On passing the site of a previous day's ambush, Union soldier Ambrose Bierce noted that the unburied dead had changed their positions. They also appeared to have thrown off some of their clothing, which lay nearby in disorder. Their expressions had an added blankness—they had no faces. As Bierce's column passed the spot, a desultory firing began. "One might have thought the living paid honors to the dead," he wrote. "No; the firing was a military execution; the condemned, a herd of galloping swine. They had eaten our fallen, but—touching magnanimity!—we did not eat theirs."[91]

Panhandling Delegates

On December 13, while battle raged on Allegheny Mountain, delegates to a constitutional convention at Wheeling fixed the territorial limits of the proposed new state of West Virginia. Forty-four counties were included unconditionally. An additional six (Pendleton, Hardy, Hampshire, Morgan, Berkeley and Jefferson) were added to form an eastern panhandle—created to place the vital Baltimore and Ohio Railroad in Union hands. Thus West Virginia became the only state in America with two panhandles![92]

Christmas in Camp

Christmas 1861 was unique for the armies. Soldiers spent the holiday season without family or loved ones. For those encamped on the mountain crests, frigid temperatures, snow and ice offered little holiday cheer. "We are *amusing* ourselves hovering around a fire in our tent, which smokes us nearly to death," Confederate James Hall noted in his diary at Camp Allegheny. "Though last night was Christmas Eve, I did not sleighride much! Instead of that, we were marched out ... on the mountain, to guard the batteries and artillery. We spent our Christmas Eve very gaily, sure."[93]

A cartoon mocks **freezing Confederates** *on Allegheny Mountain during the first winter of war.*
(*Harper's Weekly,* January 4, 1862)

1862—Strange Struggle for Statehood

Summary of Events:

Stonewall Jackson launches a winter campaign, but faces insurrection at Romney.

A Confederate draft swells the ranks of guerrillas—punishing soldiers and civilians alike.

George Crook's Union force defeats Henry Heth at Lewisburg.

Intrepid female guerrillas make their mark.

Gen. Jenkins' Rebel raiders provoke a scare.

Union Gen. Joseph Lightburn is driven from the Kanawha Valley, while his old neighbor Stonewall Jackson captures a colossal Union force at Harpers Ferry.

The West Virginia statehood bill moves to Congress, but stalls over slavery.

Senator John Carlile, former champion of statehood, tries to sabotage the bill, but "Radical Republicans" come to the rescue.

President Lincoln pulls an "Odd Trick" to create West Virginia.

Cold as the North Pole

The winter of 1861-62 was one of the worst old mountaineers could remember. Soldiers suffered terribly in fortifications on the heights of Cheat and Allegheny Mountains. Sheltered only by tents or crowded in crude cabins, hundreds were victimized by frostbite. Deep snow or ice sometimes halted all duty. "It is snowing; the wind is blowing a hurricane; it is as cold as the North Pole," reported a shivering soldier at Camp Allegheny. "I have seen ice on the barrels of our guns one fourth of an inch thick," added another; "it's almost a matter of impossibility to describe the sufferings of the soldiers on the Alleghany Mountain." Their trials were compared to the Revolutionary winter at Valley Forge.[94]

The Romney Insurrection

On New Year's Day, Confederate Gen. Stonewall Jackson, headquartered at Winchester, launched an offensive to seize Romney and prevent a junction of U.S. forces. Jackson's troops first marched north to disrupt the B&O Railroad and C&O Canal, but were punished by a fierce winter storm. Pushing on to Romney, they found that Union troops had abandoned the town. Jackson left Gen. William Loring's division in that filthy place and retired to Winchester for the winter. Loring's disgruntled officers protested to Richmond and were recalled, wiping out Jackson's efforts. Stonewall resigned from the army in a huff, but was talked out of it by authorities.[95]

Sam Watkins. *This Tennessee Confederate claimed he found a squad of sentinels frozen to death at their post!* (Company Aytch)

The "Death Watch"

During Jackson's Romney expedition, Confederates suffered horribly in the subzero cold. Sam Watkins of the 1st Tennessee Infantry wrote of a nightmarish scene as he prepared to relieve the guards on Sir Johns Run in Morgan County: "If I remember correctly, there were just eleven of them. Some were sitting down and some were lying down; but each and every one was as cold and as hard frozen as the icicles that hung from their hands and faces and clothing—dead! They had died at their post of duty."[96]

Not Impressed with Stonewall

Confederates of the Army of the Northwest were uninspired by their first sight of Stonewall Jackson. They thought his war steed "looked more like a plow horse," and laughed at how Jackson's feet were drawn up in stirrups much too short. They sneered at the "old, dingy military cap" slumped on his head, "his nose erected in the air, his old rusty sabre rattling by his side." Perturbed by Stonewall's secrecy and the trials they endured on the march to Romney, many thought him "insane" and called him "Fool Tom Jackson." Future events would prove them wrong.[97]

Sermon in a Snowstorm

A memorable sermon by Rev. James Bolton, chaplain of the 2nd (U.S.) Virginia Infantry, took place one winter morning at Camp Elkwater. The open air was the only tabernacle available. Gathering his flock near the breastworks, with a cannon as his pulpit, the chaplain launched into a spirited sermon. As the preaching progressed, a heavy snowstorm swept down the valley, but the chaplain persevered, finally closing with a flourish. Although blanketed with snow, neither he nor his flock was discomfited.[98]

Panthers Stalk the Sentinels

Soldiers on guard or "picket" duty in the wilderness were sometimes terrorized by mountain lions. Posted alone, without benefit of a fire or a torch, the picket would hear faint footfalls as darkness fell. A big cat might circle his post, snarling in a threatening manner as the petrified picket backed against a tree with his bayonet forward, for it was too dark to see or shoot. Daybreak could not come soon enough![99]

Lander's Last Dash

On February 14, Gen. Frederick Lander, intrepid hero of the battles of Philippi and Rich Mountain, launched a raid on Confederates at Bloomery Gap, Hampshire County. Unwilling to lose the element of surprise, Lander struck with cavalry before his infantry arrived. "Follow me!" Lander cried as he rode to the head of the column and charged. Routing the enemy, he cut off several Rebel officers and calmly demanded their surrender. But Lander had not recovered from a wound received months earlier, and his report on the action at Bloomery Gap included a request to be relieved: "I am too much broken to do any severe work." He died in camp at Paw Paw only two weeks later.[100]

Rev. Gordon Battelle tried to abolish slavery during West Virginia's constitutional convention, but his resolutions were voted down—too many Unionists were slaveholders! (Author's collection)

Statehood's "Holy Horror"

The constitutional convention ground to a finish at Wheeling on February 18 as members framed a constitution for the proposed new state of West Virginia. Delegates had agreed to a "proper boundary" for the new state, but were baffled when Rev. Gordon Battelle offered resolutions calling for the gradual emancipation of enslaved people. As one delegate noted, "a kind of tremor—a holy horror was visible throughout the house!" Battelle's resolutions were rejected. The delegates were well aware that many statehood advocates were also slaveholders![101]

Escape from the Athenaeum

George Deering, a "daring rebel," was imprisoned in the Wheeling Athenaeum, known by detractors as "Lincoln's Bastille." Locked up on the second floor of the building, Deering improvised a saw from a pocketknife and managed to cut a hole in the floor beneath his bed. Lowering himself down to the ground floor at night, he obtained a shovel and dug a tunnel beneath the securely bolted door leading to Market Street, enabling him to escape. Union authorities marveled at his tiny tunnel, noting how it must have afforded "a pretty tight squeeze" for the enterprising escapee.[102]

A "Sham" Skirmish

Encamped on Wheeling Island, a battalion of Connecticut cavalry had seen no real action since enlistment. Growing tired of their tedious duty, the troopers decided to indulge in a sham engagement. So spirited was their play that a horse was killed and three or four soldiers badly hurt from saber blows.[103]

Lt. Alfred Sickman, 2nd West Virginia Infantry, killed in action on Allegheny Mountain. The Confederates left his body unburied for months as a warning.
(History of the Fifth West Virginia Cavalry)

Unburied Bluecoats

Gen. Ed Johnson's Confederates withdrew from Camp Allegheny on April 2, and Union Gen. Robert Milroy occupied the works four days later. Milroy marveled at the strength of the abandoned fortress. Gruesome discoveries were made: cannonballs had been buried as booby traps inside chimney hearths; dead horses rotted in the springheads. The unburied bodies of two Union soldiers were also found. Badly decomposed, they had laid on the ground since the battle of December 13—almost four months earlier! The Confederates likely left them unburied as a warning.[104]

Beheaded by a Scythe

On April 26, a military court in Charleston found Henry Kuhl, Hamilton Windon and Conrad Kuhl guilty of the gruesome murder of a Union soldier in Braxton County. The three men had beaten the young man, forced his head into a rail fence and beheaded him with a scythe. Two of the three were sentenced to death by hanging. No one knew the poor victim's name. A young girl who witnessed the event was reportedly driven insane.[105]

Dodging the Draft

As the one-year enlistments of Southern volunteers came to a close, the Confederate government instituted a draft, the first in American history. As established on April 26, white males between the ages of 18-45 years were required to serve with a few exceptions, including the hiring of a substitute. Many men balked at this threat to liberty, and fled the armies to join the ranks of guerrillas.[106]

Recruiting the Rangers

Col. John Imboden, authorized to raise a regiment of "Partisan Rangers" by the Confederate government, issued a recruiting notice on May 8 that sought handpicked men for "adventurous service." Imboden declared: "I don't propose to rely much on military science, but mainly on great celerity of movement, sleepless vigilance, good marksmanship and plenty of old-fashioned rough fighting and bushwhacking, to make the country too hot to permit a Yankee to show his head outside of his camp."[107]

A Mistaken Mistress

The *Wheeling Daily Intelligencer* reported on the proceedings of a court martial trial at Charleston in which Captain William A. West was discharged from Union service. Among the charges against him was "keeping his wife in camp, dressed in the uniform of a soldier." The newspaper printed a retraction on May 13: "We are requested to state that this is a mistake—it was another man's wife that West had in camp, and not his own. We make the correction with pleasure."[108]

Regretting the Rangers

The Confederate legislature in Richmond passed the Partisan Ranger Act in an attempt to regulate guerrilla warfare. The effort proved futile. Commonwealth attorney William Skeen of Pocahontas County begged authorities to disband the Rangers. "Virginia has armed these men to murder, rob, steal and commit all other offenses, he informed Confederate Gen. Henry Heth at Lewisburg. "They are supreme judges of the loyalty of Virginians, and pass sentence of death or confiscation of property without evidence …" A horrified Gen. Heth disarmed two Ranger units, but the "bushwackers" continued to flourish.[109]

Rathbone's Boneheaded Truce

Col. John Rathbone, commanding the 11th West Virginia Infantry, signed a misguided truce on May 18 with guerrillas at Spencer. Guerrilla leaders George Downs, Peregrine Hays and George Silcott tricked Rathbone into believing that Union Gen. Benjamin Kelley had sanctioned the pact. Under its terms, the "Moccasin Rangers" were allowed to visit their homes and move unmolested for eight days. In addition, Dick Greathouse, a "notorious guerrilla" leader, was released from a Spencer jail. Upon learning of the pact, Gen. Kelley was furious. "Dissolve the truce at once," he instructed Rathbone, "and proceed under your orders to disperse, kill or capture the Ranger bands."[110]

John Brown's Body

A traveling newspaper editor noted the desolation at Harpers Ferry since the commencement of war. One of the notable structures not in ruins was the engine house where John Brown and his band made their ill fated stand against slavery in 1859. Ironically, Rebel prisoners were jailed there now—perhaps some who had jeered at Brown's execution. Just as the editor departed, a company of Union soldiers passed the engine house, chanting the song: "John Brown's body lies a-mouldering in the grave."[111]

An Incident at Lewisburg

The Battle of Lewisburg, a Union victory fought in the streets of that town on May 23, resulted in many casualties and a few amusing incidents. Among the latter: Confederate Joseph Rollins of the 22nd Virginia Infantry watched the battle begin just as a comrade dropped his pants to answer nature's call. As the enemy advanced, the startled soldier took off running with his pants still around his ankles. Rollins opened his mouth to laugh, and at that moment, a bullet passed through his cheeks. The timing might have saved his life. He later grew a beard to hide the scars.[112]

Saved by the Bible

A Bible saved the life of a member of the 36th Ohio Infantry at the Battle of Lewisburg. The testament was tucked in the soldier's blouse pocket, just over his heart. A bullet passed through the Bible and his clothing, stopping at the skin. He fell, but did not know what hit him until that evening, when he found the flattened ball.[113]

Antique Artillery

An antique cannon was engaged in the clash at Lewisburg. Soldiers claimed it was a relic of the American Revolution. The smoothbore 6-pounder had been taken from the Norfolk Navy Yard and drafted into Confederate service. Lacking a carriage, it was braced by fence rails and chained to a tree during the fight at Lewisburg. At one point, the gun whirled off the rails and fired a solid shot that knocked off a corner of the Methodist Church. Although recent scholarship casts doubt on much of this story, repairs to the church are still visible and the old gun remains on display in Springfield, Ohio.[114]

The Tiny "Horse Soldier"

Eleven year-old Marcellus Zimmerman reportedly "rode" a broomstick horse during the Battle of Lewisburg. Pretending he was a cavalry trooper, young Zimmerman loved to mount his broomstick steed and canter through the Union camp. He became a noted historian later in life.[115]

Rendezvous at Rosbys Rock

A meeting of the Union citizens of Marshall County was called on June 5 at Rosbys Rock. Their purpose was to raise companies of "Home Guards" to protect the citizens from guerrilla depredations. A committee was formed to petition Governor Pierpont seeking arms for defense. The people passed a resolution that "no one sympathizing with the so called Southern Confederacy shall have any protection whatever."[116]

Nancy Hart, Bushwacker

Nancy Hart was a Rebel spy and bushwacker of legendary proportions. Deadly as a venomous snake, she rode with a notorious guerrilla outfit known as the Moccasin Rangers. Arrested by Union troops in 1862, Nancy was thrown into a jail at Summersville. Dirty and unkempt, she gained the sympathy of a telegrapher, who furnished some calico,

Nancy Hart, a legendary guerrilla, "deadly as a copperhead snake."
(WV State Archives)

needles and thread. When Nancy's sewing was finished, he asked her to pose for a photograph in her new dress. Nancy had never seen a camera—she feared it was a devise for her execution! After some comforting talk, the image was made. In short order, Nancy snatched the jailor's gun, shot him dead, and rode off into legend.[117]

Snake Hunters' Drill

The Snake Hunters, an intrepid band of Unionists led by Capt. John Baggs, were a "counter irritant" to the Moccasin Rangers. Their peculiar style and reputation for daring (and drinking) reflected the colorful Capt. Baggs, a man described as "half horse, half alligator and the rest snapping turtle." Capt. Baggs gave orders in a unique and combative way: "Put down them thar blasted old guns and be d_____ to you!" (Translation: 'Stack Arms') When dismissed, the Snake Hunters broke ranks in a cacophony of "whoops, yells and squeals, interspersed with life-like imitations of birds and beasts."[118]

Ogling the Old General

Nancy Duskey, one of a family of bushwhackers, was a formidable spy and guerrilla in her own right. Arrested by Union scouts, she was taken to headquarters and interrogated by Gen. Benjamin Kelley. Nancy refused to speak, so Kelley offered some fatherly advice: "You have given the Union forces a good deal of trouble … You must quit this business Nancy, you are young and handsome and would be a good wife for some worthy man. Get married, settle down, and give us no more trouble." Nancy told him there was no worthy suitor. Kelley then offered her the pick of his staff officers. Looking them over, she retorted: "I believe I prefer the old general himself." The flattery worked—Nancy was released![119]

The "Judas" of Statehood

John S. Carlile, vocal leader of the new state movement, drafted the West Virginia statehood bill as a U.S. Senator for the Restored Government of Virginia in Washington. Submitted late in the session, Senate Bill 365 added fifteen Shenandoah Valley (Confederate) counties to the new state, emancipated slave children, and required a second constitutional convention for approval. The bill was a sham—cleverly designed to sabotage statehood! Carlile's colleagues were dumbfounded: "[W]hat change has come over the spirit of his dream I know not," declared Senator Ben Wade of Ohio, "His conversion is greater than that of St. Paul." The reasons for Carlile's flip-flop on West Virginia statehood are still debated.[120]

Tucker County Resolutions

On July 5, a group of Unionists gathered at St. George, the Tucker County seat. They resolved "that in view of recent raids of guerrillas, horse thieves, and desperadoes in the county and vicinity ... we the undersigned citizens do in good faith hereby pledge to each other our mutual aid and protection; and we further promise to frown upon all persons engaged in this diabolical work; that we will refuse them any aid or comfort whatever, and that if necessary we will unite to resist their incursions for murder and plunder by force of arms."[121]

Radicals to the Rescue

Abolitionists in the U.S. Senate, the so-called "Radical Republicans," seized upon the West Virginia statehood bill and added a clause for the *gradual* emancipation of enslaved people. This "Willey Amendment," named for the Restored Government's U.S. Senator Waitman Willey, passed the Senate on July 14 by a vote of 23-17. Senator John Carlile, the former firebrand of statehood, voted against it![122]

John Carlile led the push for West Virginia statehood, but then tried to sabotage the movement as a U.S. Senator. (loc.gov reproduction no. LCDIG-cwpbh-02706)

Carlile's Defense

Following calls for his resignation, Senator John Carlile tried to account for his attempted sabotage of West Virginia statehood in a speech at Wheeling. The *Wheeling Intelligencer* was unmoved, noting Carlile's "treachery" and his "lame, hobbling and stammering" defense. Carlile's claim that abolitionists were changing the "purpose and objects of the war" moved the *Intelligencer* to assert that this was now "an abolition war."[123]

Defiling the Flag

The arrival of Company K of the 6th West Virginia Infantry sparked a ruckus in Philippi. Offended by the Union soldiers, Helen Capito and Elisabeth McClaskey snatched the company flag from an astonished standard bearer and ripped it to shreds. The two young women were promptly arrested. Their punishment included a formal apology and the sewing of a new flag for the bluecoats. A bond was posted to ensure their future good behavior.[124]

Stifling Secessionists

Lt. Col. Daniel Frost, commanding at Ravenswood, ordered Union troops to stop all gatherings of Confederate sympathizers and the distribution of treasonable material in Jackson County. Dated July 31, the order required all travellers on business in Ravenswood to "leave before dark." All sales of the *Cincinnati Enquirer* (a secessionist newspaper) were prohibited. Finally, soldiers were instructed to seize any arms belonging to Jackson County secessionists.[125]

Flashing a Feisty Widow

Angered by the arrest of his free black servant, Lt. Henry Myers of the Ringgold (PA) Cavalry pulled a pistol and shot into the fireplace at the inn of the widow Reckner. As soldiers crowded around, Mrs. Reckner, a "very respectable lady," informed Myers that he could kill her, but would not scare her. Myers then "hauled out his tool and shook it" at Mrs. Reckner, yelling, "Maybe this will suit you." Myers was charged with "disgraceful conduct."[126]

Rousing Resolutions

A Union meeting at the Lewis County courthouse was typical of war gatherings during the summer of 1862. Congressman J. B. Blair of the Restored Government stirred the crowd with appeals to patriotism. Resolutions called for a cash bounty for recruits under President Lincoln's latest call for volunteers. The assembly groaned and hissed in condemning Senator John Carlile as a traitor. Finally, a warning to Rebel sympathizers: the "notorious John D. Imboden at the head of a large guerrilla band now on our border, threatening to destroy our property, murder and carry away captive our people ... we here declare that all destruction visited on us by this hellish band ... shall be revisited upon secession sympathizers in our midst."[127]

Jane Snyder's Ride

In August, Col. John Imboden led a force of 300 Partisan Rangers against the B&O Railroad bridges at Rowlesburg. Jane Snyder, the teenage daughter of a leader of Union home guards known as the "Swamp Dragons," learned of Imboden's raid. Mounting a fleet horse, Jane rode through the night to alert her father and a Union garrison at present-day Parsons. When halted by the sentinels, Jane gave her name, which by coincidence was the password that day. Her Paul Revere-like ride saved the Union garrison and spread an alarm that foiled Imboden.[128]

Demise of the Dapple Gray

Guerrillas ambushed a Union scouting party led by Col. Thomas Harris of the 10th West Virginia Infantry near Huttonsville. Mounted on horseback in the lead, Harris was a prominent target for the bushwackers. Miraculously, the colonel went unscathed; his horse, although mortally wounded, somehow carried its rider to safety. This beautiful stallion, a "fine dapple gray," was the very animal that carried Maj. Gen. George McClellan safely through the First Campaign.[129]

Heard It Through the Grapevine

During big battles in the Shenandoah Valley and eastern Virginia, citizens along the eastern margins of the proposed new state could sometimes hear the distant sound of conflict. Lying down with an ear to the ground, they listened raptly to the faint "rumble" of artillery. If the news was slow to arrive, they could reliably assume that the Confederates had been victorious.[130]

Fought for Both Sides

Granville Phillips of Barbour County enlisted as a Confederate soldier in the First Partisan Rangers (62nd Virginia Infantry) on August 26, but deserted during a raid three months later. Phillips joined the 6th West Virginia Infantry in 1864. He was one of a surprising number of residents who fought for both the Union *and* Confederate armies during the Civil War![131]

Granville Phillips *fought in both the Union and Confederate armies. Can you guess which uniform he wears in this image?* (Author's collection)

The Hard Hand of War

A letter from Lt. H. W. Brazie, 9th West Virginia Infantry: "You hear and read of the valor and glorious deeds of the army, but do not know the suffering and destruction that follows where an army moves. When you see women and children driven from their homes without any of their property … and made to witness their homes … burned before their eyes, you may think it hard; but the most affecting sight was, when we fell back, to see whole families trying to escape from the enemy … Little babies in their mother's arms, and others from three to ten years old, trying to keep up."[132]

Dead Man Walking

Confederate raiders under Gen. Albert Gallatin Jenkins entered Buckhannon on August 30, drove out the defenders and seized valuable ordnance. Among the dead was a citizen named Andrew Black. Black's body was laid on a table in the Baptist church with pennies over his eyes. While working nearby a few hours later, surgeon J. R. Blair heard the pennies drop to the floor and turned to see Black sitting up. Terrified, Blair bolted outside. Convincing himself that Black's actions were merely a reflex, Blair returned to find the stiffened corpse lying on the floor, several steps away from the table![133]

Bodacious Burglars

More than a million dollars (worth at least $25 million today) was housed in the vault of the Wheeling Custom House. On the night of September 3, a daring burglary came close to breaching the vault. Secreting themselves in the building at closing time, burglars chiseled a hole through bricks, concrete and iron reinforcing bands. Viewing the treasure trove in the vault below, they tried to fish bags of money out with a hook. Daybreak forced the robbers to abandon their work, leaving tools and an empty bottle of whiskey in the auditor's office.[134]

Cheering the Enemy

During the Maryland Campaign, Gen. Robert E. Lee divided his army and sent a large force under Gen. Thomas "Stonewall" Jackson to eliminate the Union garrison at Harpers Ferry. Jackson deftly occupied high ground surrounding the town, planted artillery and shelled the Union garrison into submission on September 15, capturing 12,500 Union soldiers and 73 pieces of artillery—the largest surrender of U.S. troops during the Civil War. Union prisoners, disgusted by the leadership of their own commanders, doffed their caps and cheered Jackson as the Confederate general rode past their camp.[135]

Wedding Bell Blues

George W. Printz, a Union telegraph operator in the town of Beverly, fell madly in love with Harriett Crawford, the young daughter of a prominent family living there. But Miss Harriett would not think of marrying a "Yankee." She consented to wed Printz after the war was over—if he would agree to join the Confederate cause. Bowing to the "mightiest power under Heaven," Printz deserted and fled south to the Rebel army. After the war, he returned to Beverly and Harriet Crawford married him as promised.[136]

John Packham, a twelve year-old fifer in the Union army, was shot for refusing to surrender at the Battle of Fayetteville. He received a medal for bravery.
(*Frank Leslie's Illustrated,* November 8, 1862)

The Boy Hero

John Packham was only 12 years old when he enlisted as a fifer in the 34th Ohio Infantry. At the Battle of Fayetteville on September 10, a Confederate soldier, seeking information, yelled at Packham: "You little red-top devil (Packham wore a colorful zouave uniform), come over here or I'll kill you." Packham refused. Again the Rebel cried out, and again Packham said no. Another Rebel advanced and called out: "you little fool, we won't hurt you if you come over. We only want to talk to you." The little hero answered: "I know what you want. I can't come," whereupon the Rebel took aim and wounded the little fellow in the knee. Comrades carried Packham off the field. For his bravery, the young soldier received a medal.[137]

Lost Cannon of Cotton Hill

A persistent tale claims that Confederate forces abandoned a cannon on the steep slopes overlooking Gauley Bridge. For more than a century, relic hunters, Boy Scout troops and civic leaders have searched for the elusive gun, occasionally turning up a Civil War cannonball to spark renewed interest. Historians have dismissed the story as nothing more than a myth, but the search continues![138]

Flight of the "Contrabands"

In the Battle of Charleston on September 13, a large force of Confederates under Gen. William Loring drove Union Col. Joseph Lightburn's defenders from the Kanawha Valley. Seizing a local newspaper press, Loring published a broadsheet declaring that the Confederates had come "to rescue the people from the despotism of the counterfeit State Government imposed on you by Northern bayonets." Not everyone agreed. Enslaved African-Americans fled as "contraband" with Union soldiers toward Ohio in a quest for freedom.[139]

A Flotilla of Refugees

During Union Col. Lightburn's retreat from the Kanawha Valley, Victoria Hansford marveled at the scene near Charleston. Boats of every size filled the Kanawha River, stretching as far as the eye could see. Union sympathizers fled downstream in a flotilla of flat boats, skiffs and canoes. A person could almost cross the river by jumping from one boat to the next. One poor couple had fashioned a makeshift raft of planks. Water splashed over them as the husband paddled. Their property was piled into a washtub at one end and the wife sat at the other end in a rocking chair.[140]

Guarded by his Brothers

Three young Confederates belonging to John Imboden's command were captured and imprisoned in the Athenaeum at Wheeling. One of them, Cyrus M. Dent, found two of his brothers standing guard over him. The brothers were members of a West Virginia regiment.[141]

Unwelcome in Charlestown

In October, Union troops occupying Charlestown found their welcome less than cordial. A *New York Times* correspondent noted: "At noon we entered the village, and for the fifth time during the war ... But how different our reception from that given us in Frederick, Sharpsburg, and other Maryland towns. Not a flag flying, except the yellow index of the hospitals. Doors, blinds and windows closed, curtains drawn, and the few residents visibly staring silently and sullenly at us. They looked even less kind than the rebel wounded ... There was no other smile or friendly greeting, except from the negroes, who welcomed us."[142]

Spying on the Prisoners

A prisoner sent to Camp Chase in Columbus, Ohio, was in reality a spy on "secret service." As directed by Governor Pierpont, Washington Cline was to mingle with prisoners from Marion County to gain intelligence on "horse-stealing, depredations on private property" and other mischief plaguing the region. When finished, he was instructed to take the oath of allegiance and report to authorities in Wheeling.[143]

Angry Abolitionist

Union Gen. Robert Milroy, a fiery abolitionist in command at Clarksburg, issued General Orders No. 28 on October 22: "The General Commanding has been repeatedly pained to learn that a few bad men in some of the regiments of his command are in the habit of abusing, beating, and otherwise mistreating the negro and mullato servants and teamsters ... These black people are generally quiet and orderly: they were created black and cannot help it: they have mostly been made slaves, and robbed of the proceeds of their own labor ... and have left their traitor masters ... and are desirous of helping us all they can ... It is therefore ordered and hereby made the duty of *every officer and soldier* of this command to *immediately shoot down*" anyone abusing or mistreating them.[144]

Invented the Machine Gun?

Confederates John and Marshall Wood of the 22nd Virginia Infantry were known as brilliant inventors. The two were authorized to work on a rapid-fire weapon during the brief stay of Gen. Loring's army at Charleston. When the Confederates fell back on October 9, they were forced to abandon their bulky "machine gun" in the Kanawha River. The pair met later with Richard Gatling, who was reportedly interested in a partnership. Ultimately, he got credit for inventing the "Gatling gun."[145]

*Union **General Robert Milroy** ordered disloyal citizens to pay a fine or be shot! His "assessment" sparked outrage and disbelief at the highest levels of government.* (Author's collection)

A "Diabolical" Assessment

Daring raids by John Imboden's Partisan Rangers, coupled with defiant behavior by Tucker County secessionists, moved Union Gen. Robert Milroy to issue a chilling order known as the "Assessment." This "wicked and shameful" act was levied on Southern sympathizers to pay for Imboden's deeds. Failure to pay the Assessment would enact a grim penalty: *"their houses will be burned and themselves shot, and their property all seized."* News of Milroy's order sparked outrage and disbelief at the highest levels of government. Authorities in Washington cancelled the order, but not before the Confederate legislature placed a $100,000 bounty on Milroy's head![146]

The Glamour of Guerrillas

The romantic image of the bushwhackers played well in metropolitan Richmond. By December, citizens were treated to a play entitled "The Guerrillas." Written by James D. McCabe, Jr., it was the first original drama produced in the Confederacy. The story was set in the mountains of "Western" Virginia. The heroes were an alluring band of bushwackers who protected the defenseless citizens from Yankee depredations—and their "lecherous designs" on Virginia's fair maidens.[147]

Whipped for their Sins

A letter from "A Rebel" at Princeton told of the suffering and demoralization of the Confederate army as winter set in: "The soldier freezes in the tented field and his destitute family both freeze and starve at home unheeded and uncared for." Southern soldiers began to desert. A deserter named Payne was punished thusly: his head was shaved, his thigh branded with the letter "D," and then he was drummed out of camp. Six deserters who had been caught "were publicly whipped" for the offense.[148]

A "Daring, Brilliant" Raid

In a blinding snowstorm on November 26, Maj. William H. Powell and twenty troopers of the 2nd West Virginia Cavalry raided a camp of five hundred Confederate cavaliers in Sinking Creek Valley, Greenbrier County. Finding the camp poorly guarded, Powell put spurs to his horse and led a charge that captured or dispersed the whole Rebel force without firing a shot! In hindsight, Union Gen. George Crook called this expedition "one of the most daring, brilliant and successful of the whole war." The controversial Powell was awarded the Medal of Honor for his exploit.[149]

Undercover Operative

A young soldier in a tight-fitting cavalry uniform was arrested in Charleston and jailed as a suspected spy. Under interrogation, "Harry Fitzallen" was found to be a woman! Born in Scotland, she had trained as an actress and even played the role of a prostitute. Calling herself Marian McKenzie, she had gone into the service solely for "the love of excitement" and claimed to have enlisted in regiments of both armies. She was furnished with women's clothing as the provost marshal investigated her claims.[150]

Lincoln's "Odd Trick"

Following passage of the West Virginia Statehood bill by Congress, President Abraham Lincoln's cabinet debated the merits of the measure. Lincoln questioned the constitutionality of West Virginia statehood and withheld his signature as the bill's deadline loomed on December 31, 1862. Legend holds that Congressman Jacob Blair crawled through a White House window early on New Year's Day to learn the bill's fate. Lincoln greeted him in bedclothes, smiling as he displayed the statehood parchment with his signature![151]

President Lincoln *claimed West Virginia statehood was "expedient" for the Union war effort, regardless of its constitutionality.* (National Archives Identifier: 527722)

1863—Raids, Refugees, and Emancipation

Summary of Events:

Unionists cheer West Virginia statehood and the Emancipation Proclamation, but Rebels and "Copperheads" condemn both measures.

A new governor is crowned.

The bushwhacker's war grows more brutal.

In a year of raids, Confederates under Jones and Imboden rampage across the new state, while Wheeling legislators arm to confront John Hunt Morgan.

Union Gen. William Averell battles for law books at White Sulphur Springs, and "Mudwall" Jackson's Confederates are stymied at Bulltown.

Brothers square off in the epic Battle of Droop Mountain.

Averell launches a raid on Salem, Virginia, fools a renowned cast of Confederate generals, and backtracks to Beverly in time for Christmas dinner.

Emancipation!

On New Year's Day, 1863, Union Gen. Robert Milroy's division was on the march toward Winchester. Halting on the summit of North Mountain in a snowstorm, Milroy addressed the troops:

"[Men] don't you know that this is Emancipation Day, when all slaves will be made free? This day President Lincoln will proclaim the freedom of four millions of human slaves, the most important event in the history of the world since Christ was born. Our boast that this is a land of liberty has been a flaunting lie ... the defeats of our armies in the past we have deserved, because we waged a war to protect and perpetuate ... the chains of slavery. Hereafter we shall prosecute the war to establish and perpetuate liberty for all mankind ... and the Lord God Almighty will fight on our side ... and the Union armies will triumph. Three cheers for the proclamation!" The air filled with wild shouts.[152]

Statehood's Strange Bedfellow

As the Emancipation Proclamation went into effect, celebrations erupted across the new state at the news of Lincoln's signing of the West Virginia statehood bill. Cannons and volleys of musketry blasted salutes; West Virginia Union soldiers paraded the streets of Wheeling, Weston and other towns. Lost in all the pomp was a curious fact: not all enslaved people in the new state would gain freedom. The Emancipation Proclamation did not apply to West Virginia, and the statehood bill passed by Congress called only for the *gradual* emancipation of slaves.[153]

Stealing the Sheriff

Ordered to disrupt the Pierpont Government, Confederate Partisan Rangers kidnapped Barbour County sheriff James Trayhern on the 4th of January. Governor Pierpont responded by ordering the arrest of eight Barbour County secessionists—all to be held until Trayhern's release. In retaliation, Col. John Imboden threatened to imprison "every man I can lay my hands upon, who holds any office under the usurped State of West Virginia." He pledged to execute two prisoners "of the highest rank" as retaliation for the killing of two Barbour County citizens by Union soldiers. Ultimately, Trayhern was freed and no one was executed, but these threats inflamed the partisan passions.[154]

A Perfect She-Devil

Mary Jane Green, an illiterate, profane and perfectly fearless Braxton County teen, had a history of arrest by Union authorities. Described as "a perfect she-devil," her specialty was cutting Union telegraph lines. When asked why she had stuck one end of the telegraph wire into the ground, Mary Jane replied that "a great many Yankees had been killed, and as that wire pointed the way they had gone it would doubtless be used to know if there was room for more."[155]

Unclaimed Corpse

The body of a soldier, embalmed in a metal casket, appeared at the Express office in Wheeling. Unclaimed for several days, it was stowed away to avoid any offense of sight or smell. A gentleman finally arrived to claim the corpse—that of a soldier killed at Antietam. The deceased formerly lived near Sistersville, had been buried on the battlefield near Sharpsburg, and was disinterred months ago.[156]

Ordered to Do It

On a cold, snowy night in January, Union cavalrymen entered the home of Austin Handley, "one of the most esteemed" citizens of Greenbrier County. According to a complaint by Confederate Maj. Gen. Sam Jones, Handley, his wife and their young children were driven outside in their bedclothes and forced to stand barefoot in the snow. Their fine home and all the contents—furniture, clothing, private papers and money—were promptly put to the torch. A barn, stables, horses and forage were also destroyed by fire. When Handley begged for an explanation, a Yankee told him "they were ordered to do it."[157]

Slept with the Senator

A large crowd met on February 4 at the Ohio County courthouse, opposed to the new state of West Virginia. Mr. Richardson, a candidate for the Constitutional Convention, spoke passionately against the new state. He railed against emancipation, the suspension of habeas corpus, and the "black tide of tyranny." He savaged Governor Pierpont and other statehood figures. But he heaped particular scorn on Senator Ben Wade of Ohio, a leading abolitionist. "Ben Wade," said Richardson, "stinks in the night like a rotten mackerel. His feet stink, his mouth stinks, and his teeth stink. I know this for I have slept with him. Not of my own choice, for it was in a sleeping car on a railroad train."[158]

Copperheads Condemn Statehood

On February 18, the West Virginia Constitutional Convention unanimously approved the Willey Amendment's clause for the gradual emancipation of slaves. As the date for citizen ratification drew near, opponents of statehood became more vocal. These "Copperheads" or "Peace Democrats" supported the Union, but not the abolition of slavery—or the fact that Congress had dictated it. They believed in "The Constitution As It Is" and restoration of "The Union As It Was." Senator John Carlile, former Congressman Sherrard Clemens and Delegate John J. Davis were among the leading Copperheads in West Virginia, but the movement was national in scope.[159]

Dodging the Flag

Some Wheeling women of questionable loyalty were in the habit of making a point to walk around the American flag posted above a recruiting station, rather than pass beneath its folds. So distressed was the officer in charge that he stretched two flags across the sidewalk and beyond, forcing the protesting ladies into the dirty street![160]

A Rotten Egg

"New State" meetings were held across West Virginia as the referendum on the Willey Amendment approached. A meeting at Middlebourne, Tyler County, grew heated as former Congressman Sherrard Clemens spoke in opposition to the new state. Someone threw a rotten egg that missed Clemens but hit a wall, splattering his clothing. Angered, Clemens drew a revolver and pointed it at the crowd. At that, Union soldiers in the audience drew pistols on Clemens, forcing him to surrender his weapon. Passions were "fully aroused" as citizens prepared for the March 26 vote on the new state constitution.[161]

Seizing Scows and Skiffs

In order to regulate the movement of people and goods across the Potomac River from the "mouth of the Monocacy to Sir Johns Run" near Berkeley Springs, Union authorities issued an order that all must pass for inspection at Harpers Ferry or Point of Rocks, Maryland. Furthermore, citizens could not cross at any other point without a pass from headquarters. Commanding officers were ordered to seize all "boats, scows and skiffs and other watercraft" within the district to prevent illicit commerce among the Rebels.[162]

Statehood in a Landslide

Despite last-ditch efforts by Senator John Carlile and other opponents of statehood, citizens voted to ratify the new state constitution on March 26 by an overwhelming margin: 28,321-572. U.S. soldiers cast 7,696 of those votes. It was clear that Copperheads and Confederate sympathizers had boycotted the election, despite Governor Pierpont's pledge that Union soldiers at polling places were there only to maintain order, not to intimidate (the voting was by voice).[163]

A Sign of the Times

Federal court convened in Wheeling as Judge Jackson admonished the grand jury to exclude all "fear, favor or affection" in their work. Mr. John Bender was arraigned on a charge of stealing government clothing. Peter Beaver, a soldier, was arraigned on the charge of passing counterfeit gold dollars in Preston County. John L. Bonham was indicted for treason; his defense attorney claimed he was now living in New York—"far away from temptations"—and would not be likely to offend again. The Court stated that if the party resided in New York, "he was rather in the center of temptation than far away from it." A $1,000 bond was posted to ensure he kept the peace.[164]

Craving Stogies and Snuff

A scouting foray by the 8th West Virginia Infantry and "Kelley Lancers" of the 1st West Virginia Cavalry resulted in an ambush by guerrillas on the Greenbrier River in Pocahontas County. Fortunately, the bushwackers were poor shots; articles of clothing were riddled with bullet holes, and horses took hits, but only two troopers received wounds. The soldiers spent a stormy night in the Alleghenies, sustained by Marsh Wheeling "stogies" and "scotch snuff."[165]

Two Bad Apples

Elizabeth "Peg Leg" Hays and Jennie De Hart arrived in Wheeling on April 20, under arrest for spying and other indiscretions. Decamping from a steamboat, the women created quite a sensation on the streets. Miss De Hart, "a red-headed vixenish looking female," was very drunk. She cursed the abolitionists, swung her bonnet overhead, and stormed about in a fury. She struck the soldier guarding her, until he was compelled to push her away with the point of his bayonet.[166]

Grumble's Great Raid

On April 20, President Lincoln issued a proclamation stating that West Virginia would soon become the nation's thirty-fifth state. That day, Confederates launched the Jones-Imboden Raid, an ambitious effort to dismantle the new state government, wreck B&O Railroad bridges and secure horses and cattle for Robert E. Lee's army. Gens.

William "Grumble" Jones and John Imboden moved in multiple columns, sparking mayhem, panic and rumors of an invasion of Pennsylvania. For nearly a month, they pillaged across a broad swath of the state with only minor resistance. Astonished, Union General-in-Chief Henry Halleck wired from Washington: "The enemy seems to march more rapidly than we move by rail."[167]

Yankees in a Box

Grumble Jones' Rebels stormed a log blockhouse sheltering Union soldiers on April 25 at Greenland Gap. When asked why he had strayed from his command, a Confederate of White's Battalion replied: "I heard that General Jones had some Yankees up here in a box and you fellows were going to take the lid off, so I thought I would go along." He was killed in the ensuing fight.[168]

I Shot the Sheriff

Confederate Capt. French Harding shot Jesse Phares, the "bogus" (Union) sheriff of Randolph County, as Imboden's raiders closed on the town of Beverly. Phares managed to stay in the saddle and gamely rode on to sound the alarm. Upon capturing the town, Harding visited the wounded sheriff and found him doing well. The two men later became friends.[169]

Morgantown's Defiant Dames

News of the approach of Grumble Jones' Rebel raiders threw the residents of Morgantown into a panic. The spring term of circuit court broke up as thousands fled north, including U.S. Senator Waitman Willey. Accepting the surrender of the town, Jones's Confederates cut down a large United States flag at the courthouse. When the Morgantown women were cajoled to provide music, they defiantly offered the "Star Spangled Banner!"[170]

Looked Like My Sister

A ragtag group of armed citizens and Union soldiers tried to fend off Grumble Jones' raiders on April 29 at Fairmont. Fighting tenaciously until surrounded, they finally waved a white flag of surrender that looked suspiciously like a petticoat! It was only fitting, as a number of those resolute defenders were women. Shot from his horse, a mortally wounded Confederate claimed that the woman who pulled the trigger "was young and pretty and looked like my sister."[171]

Burning "Oiltown"

The most dramatic episode of the Jones-Imboden raid took place at Burning Springs, Wirt County, at the largest producing oil field in the world. Grumble Jones' raiders set fire to wells, tanks, barrels, engine houses and boats filled with oil. Explosions rocked "Oiltown" as clouds of thick black smoke filled the sky. As darkness fell on May 9, the Little Kanawha River was in flames, a "sheet of fire" coursing downstream for miles. An estimated 150,000 barrels of oil were destroyed—the first wartime destruction of an oil field in history. A witness recalled: "It looked like hell had been brought to earth."[172]

Charged with Treason

Shamed by the success of Jones' raiders, Union Gen. Benjamin Roberts determined to remove all Confederate sympathizers from his district. Disloyal families were rounded up and sent across the lines to "Dixie," or charged with treason and delivered to Northern prison camps. Dr. Thomas Camden of Weston and his family, including an infant son, were forced to leave their home and belongings behind and move to Camp Chase prison in Columbus, Ohio. Dr. Camden recalled in disgust: "It reminded us of the children of Israel going into captivity."[173]

A Gifted Gunner

Sergeant Milton Humphreys, an eighteen year-old Greenbrier County native, was a mathematical prodigy. Just two months after enlisting in Bryan's (Virginia) Battery of Confederate artillery, Humphreys accomplished something new to warfare—indirect fire. At the Battle of Fayetteville on May 19, Humphreys tucked his cannon behind a grove of trees and bombarded a Union fort he could not see. Using trigonometry and a spotter, he rained fire on an enemy who had no idea where the shells were coming from. Humphreys claimed no credit for an invention "so obvious."[174]

Government in Exile

On May 28, the new State of West Virginia held its first election of officers. A "Union State Ticket" had been chosen at Parkersburg on May 6, in the shadow of Grumble Jones' raiders. Candidates on the ticket were unopposed in the general election, but no returns were received from fifteen counties under Confederate control—almost one third of the new state! Arthur Boreman of Wood County was elected as the first governor of West Virginia. Frank Pierpont, leader of the "Restored Government," had declined the honor. Pierpont prepared to move his Restored Government of Virginia to Union-controlled Alexandria. Although considered the "Father of West Virginia," Pierpont never served as governor of the state.[175]

No Rebel Images

The Provost Marshal seized all pictures of Confederate army officers and officials displayed at the various photograph galleries in Wheeling. This was deemed advisable due to the concern that "these pictures afforded a great deal of gratification" to Rebel sympathizers in the region.[176]

Inauguration Day

June 20, the official first day of West Virginia statehood, was marked with ceremonies, military parades and fireworks. Thousands gathered in Wheeling as Governor Pierpont delivered an address in front of Linsly Institute, the temporary capitol. Pierpont told the crowd his Restored Government of *Virginia* was moving to Alexandria to suppress the rebellion. He asked them to guard their "*sacred liberties*" and to "Fight as long as a mountain presents a site for a battery—or a grotto remains to serve as a rifle pit." Bidding them adieu, he introduced Governor-elect Arthur Boreman to thunderous applause.[177]

Letter From a Rebel Girl

A letter from a Braxton County girl to a Union soldier: "Dear Sir—this is to inform you that I ... received your letter ... [B]efore there can be a correspondent between you and me, I would like to know whether you have a wife and family or not. I heard the married men of the 3d 'Virginia Regt' would Spark a heap quicker than the young men would. You said you was happy with your acquaintance with me ... if you had been in Dixie your letter might have been welcome ... You know as Strong a 'Secesh' as I am don't want to have any thing to Say to a 'Yankee' ... I thought you would have more respect for me than to kill my brother as you said you would ... you on one side me on the other, it wouldn't do ... Sending you my love if you was a 'Secesh' ... But [I] remain a rebel Until Death. Hurraw for Jeff [Davis], R. C."[178]

The Unlucky Thirteen

Confederate Col. William L. Jackson launched an aborted raid on Beverly (July 2-3) that proved embarrassing to Union Col. Thomas M. Harris, commander of the post. In retaliation, Harris arrested a large number of local citizens and lined them up in front of the Beverly courthouse. Pacing along the line, he asked each one: "Are you a Union Man?" Those answering in the negative were ordered to take two steps forward. In all, thirteen men stepped forward, including two who claimed to be "Constitutional Union men." The unlucky thirteen were promptly sent to Fort Delaware, a Federal prison camp on Pea Patch Island. All but three ultimately died from the foul water and squalid conditions of their imprisonment.[179]

A Severe Sanction

Horse theft became a serious problem as the war progressed. Armies routinely "impressed" horses for military use. Southern sympathizers and guerrillas often stole horses and sold them to the Confederates. Some thieves took horses north to Pennsylvania or Maryland, sold them and then filed claims against the U.S. government for their "loss." The problem grew to the point where the West Virginia State Senate debated "making the crime of horse stealing punishable by death."[180]

Robbing the Paymaster

Major Doddridge, the U.S. Paymaster lodging at the McLure House in Wheeling, left his room for a few moments on business. A key remained in the lock of his safe. His movements must have been watched, for during that brief absence someone entered the room, unlocked the safe and removed $900 in "greenbacks." One of the chambermaids recalled seeing "a strange man" lurking about. Later, a bellboy discovered forty dollars, wrapped inside a sergeant's pass in a common restroom. The sergeant was held for questioning, but he was not the man seen by the maid.[181]

Tenacious Troopers!

Elements of the 2nd West Virginia Cavalry joined the 34th Ohio Volunteer (mounted) Infantry on a twelve-day expedition from Camp Piatt (present-day Belle) on the Kanawha River. Following Coal River, they crossed the mountains to Oceana and Raleigh Court-House. Along the way, they clashed with enemy forces, burned houses, and seized arms, ordnance, and quartermaster stores. During a charge through the streets of Wytheville, Virginia, Col. William Powell was felled by a pistol shot, Maj. John Hoffman thrown violently from his horse, and Col. John Toland killed. Despite their loss of leaders, the party returned to Camp Piatt in good order twelve days and some four hundred miles later.[182]

Thankless Service

Michael Quinlan of Wheeling joined the "Shriver Grays" and served many months of Confederate service in the Stonewall Brigade. Finally discharged due to poor health, he returned home and was promptly arrested by a U.S. Marshal and indicted for treason![183]

Abused by Her Jailer

Maggie Reed, a saucy young woman from Buckhannon, was arrested and confined in the Ohio County jail for spying and "manufacturing and assisting to fling to the breeze a rebel flag." When the jailer attempted to move her for making too much noise, she resisted. Infuriated, he struck her with a pistol, kicked her and dragged her by the hair to the new cell, where he whipped her. A doctor and other witnesses confirmed her testimony. The jailer was charged with mistreatment. Two female witnesses testified that Maggie had frequently used abusive language directed at the jailer and his wife—"language too gross to be repeated by a lady even upon a witness stand."[184]

Gunboat Diplomacy

As word spread that John Hunt Morgan's Confederate raiders were closing in, Ohio River communities flew into a panic. Bells rang in the city of Wheeling to sound the alarm. New recruits were summoned, and the militia called out. Members of the West Virginia legislature hastily formed a company and took up arms. Boarding a gunboat armed with cannons, they steamed up the Ohio, gallantly pursuing an enemy who did not appear.[185]

Marching with a Baby

A soldier in a Pennsylvania regiment stood out sharply on the march. Standing fully six foot-three inches tall, he carried a musket in one hand and a well-stuffed knapsack on his back. Cradled in his other arm was a four month-old "negro" baby. The child, reportedly picked up in Hampshire County, beamed at onlookers, while the soldier marched in a solemn manner, "as if going to a funeral."[186]

Battle of the "Graybacks"

A fierce engagement took place on the morning of August 10 at Wheeling's Athenaeum Prison. Bunks were carried into the middle of the street and guards opened upon the enemy with water from a fire hose. The foe included "myriads of vermin of various kinds" that had long infested the prison. The engagement lasted some four hours and resulted in the rout of "the bed bugs, body lice and other enemies" of the inmates.[187]

Sharing the Love

An attractive young woman was sent away to Camp Chase Prison in Columbus, Ohio. She had a husband in the Union army and had gone to visit him several months earlier, but became "demoralized." It was alleged that she had "dispensed her affections generally throughout the camp." She was taken away for the good of the service.[188]

A Battle for Law Books

The Battle of White Sulphur Springs (August 26-27) was a "queer" fight that went by several names: the Battle of Rocky Gap, Battle of Dry Creek and Battle of Howard's Creek. Union Gen. William Averell's Fourth Separate Brigade sought the law library of the Virginia Supreme Court of Appeals at Lewisburg for the new West Virginia government. Averell's raiders were defeated in the battle for law books, but he went on to invent an asphalt paving process that made him wealthy.[189]

Asleep on the Field

Capt. Robert Pollock, 14th Pennsylvania Cavalry, failed to obey an order to charge with his company during the Battle of White Sulphur Springs. After Union Gen. Averell's raiders withdrew from the field, Confederates found Pollock sound asleep in the rear![190]

Gagging at the Greenbrier

While Col. George Patton led Confederates at the Battle of White Sulphur Springs, his wife and son listened to the guns from a cottage nearby at the Greenbrier resort. As casualties arrived at the Greenbrier, Sue Patton rolled up her sleeves and tended to the wounded. Her seven-year-old son George recalled "following my mother around with a bucket and sponge. The smell was so awful that my mother fainted and had to be carried out."[191]

"Mudwall" Jackson?

In contrast to his famous cousin "Stonewall" Jackson, Confederate Col. William L. Jackson earned a less flattering nickname. While pursuing Gen. Averell's raiders from White Sulphur Springs, Confederates found "Mudwall Jackon" written on the walls of the courthouse at Huntersville. A Confederate trooper reminisced: "We called him 'Mudwall' in contradistinction from Stonewall Jackson," because Averell "always without an exception ran over him, knocked him down and ran him off." In fairness, many knew the future general as a "gallant and competent" officer.[192]

A Close Shave

On September 11, McNeill's Rangers and allied Confederates launched a surprise raid on Union forces at Moorefield that netted almost 150 prisoners and much-need ordnance and equipment. This "brilliant little affair" turned the tables on a superior Union force preparing to launch a raid of its own. Capt. John "Hanse" McNeill was among the few Confederate casualties. An enemy bullet shaved the skin under McNeill's nose, neatly trimming his mustache![193]

Murdered in the Outhouse

A band of thirty guerrillas, including Jim Greathouse and Wylie Dick, raided a Roane County home looking for Union soldiers. Two members of the 9th and 11th West Virginia Infantry were found asleep in the outhouse and summarily executed. Moving to another residence, the guerrillas tried to kidnap a slave girl, but she resisted and was murdered. In retaliation, Union troops killed two men charged with aiding the guerrillas. A newspaper report claimed "there can be no peace in Roane County after this outbreak until one or the other of the parties are exterminated."[194]

Unrepentant Rebel

Maggie Murphy, a vivacious teen of the "secesh persuasion," was arrested near Clarksburg and charged with attempting to burn a bridge on the Northwestern Virginia Railroad. She denied the charge, but pledged to do "all she could to aid those in arms in the South." She was sent to Camp Chase prison, her fourth incarceration since the war commenced.[195]

Balking at Bulltown

During the Battle of Bulltown (October 13), Confederate Col. William "Mudwall" Jackson's raiders surrounded a little Union garrison led by Capt. William Mattingly of the 6th West Virginia Infantry. Jackson urged surrender. Mattingly replied, "come and take us." Hours later, after heavy fire from small arms and a "jackass battery" (cannons carried on pack mules), Jackson again demanded surrender. Mattingly lay wounded, but Capt. James Simpson shot back: "I will fight until hell freezes over and then fight on the ice." The defenders held their ground; Jackson finally withdrew.[196]

Stubborn Civilian

Moses Cunningham, a "local character" living on the Bulltown battlefield, cheered the Confederates during that fight until struck by a bullet. The wound did little to deter him. After treatment by a Union surgeon, Cunningham continued to "hurrah for Jeff Davis." Reputedly threatened with death by Union soldiers, he roared above the gunfire: "Hark the tomb, a doleful sound, my ears attend the cries; Ye living men come view the ground where you d___ Yankees must shortly lie."[197]

Beheaded by a Train

On October 24, the wife of State Auditor Samuel Crane was walking along the railroad tracks at Ritchietown (South Wheeling). As an express train drew near, the engineer yelled for her to get out of the way. Alarmed and confused, she tripped over multiple tracks and fell upon the main line. The engine wheels passed directly over her neck, severing the head from her body. Horrified citizens mourned the "terrible accident."[198]

The Ghost Army

Moses Dwyer and others witnessed a remarkable scene from his porch, a few miles west of Lewisburg. In the valley beyond, thousands of men came into view, marching in strict order. They were uniformly dressed in white shirts and pants, but without guns, swords or other weapons. On they came for nearly an hour, finally passing out of sight to the north. An almost identical scene was witnessed on October 14 by Confederate pickets and "respectable citizens" at Bunger's Mill.[199]

Freeing Families of Slaves

The West Virginia Senate met on October 29 and debated various bills and resolutions. Among them was a bill to reorganize the militia. Another resolution sought to free the families of slaves who had volunteered for service in the Union army. Sadly, that topic was tabled without further discussion.[200]

Drama on Droop Mountain

The Battle of Droop Mountain (November 6), one of the most consequential fights of the war in West Virginia, was a caldron of oddities. Union Gen. William Averell's defeat of Gen. John Echols marked the beginning of the end of Confederate efforts to control the new state. West Virginia-born officers led troops on both sides; many natives squared off in a true "brother's fight." While Harrison Dye of the 22nd Virginia Infantry waited in the Confederate trenches on

Droop Mountain, his brother Frank climbed the slopes to attack with a West Virginia regiment.[201]

A Dreadful Discovery

After the fight on Droop Mountain, a Union soldier gathered some mementoes—a pencil, book, and letter found on the corpse of a member of the 14th Virginia Cavalry. The Yankee later stopped at a home in Frankford and engaged a young woman in conversation. He bragged about the trophies he had pilfered from the dead Rebel. The woman asked to see them. After a brief look, she screamed in horror—the book was owned by her brother, and the letter was one she had written to him![202]

Droop Mountain Ghosts

Numerous ghost stories surround the Battle of Droop Mountain. One night in 1920, logger Edgar Walton camped on the battlefield near the graves of Confederate dead. While tending a campfire, Walton heard leaves rustling and saw the apparition of a headless Confederate soldier float by. Others have reported ghostly screams, the sounds of battle and other soldierly specters.[203]

Gen. Henry Wise *swore he never fought under the Confederate flag—only under the banner of Virginia!*
(Author's collection)

Goggle-eyed in Gettysburg

On November 19, a delegation that included Governors Boreman and Pierpont attended the dedication of the national cemetery at Gettysburg. A reporter noted that they toured the battlefield as well. Near Spangler's Spring, they observed the Confederate dead (segregated from the Union cemetery), buried "in heaps" in shallow trenches. Signs of battle were everywhere: "Trees a foot thick had been torn off by crashing cannon balls." The reporter could not say enough about the "grand" two-hour oration by former Secretary of State Edward Everett. The short speech by President Lincoln—celebrated today as the "Gettysburg Address"—received scant mention![204]

Feeding the Famished

Kanawha Valley citizens were so impoverished by army depredations that Union Gen. Benjamin Kelley was moved to act. Special Orders No. 72 directed that foodstuffs and other "subsistence stores" be issued to the families of soldiers in U.S. service, refugees, and the families of certain political prisoners. The chief commissary of the Department of West Virginia was ordered to distribute rations and other necessities to such "destitute persons."[205]

Lawsuit Over a Slave

The case of Higgs vs. Goshorn in Wheeling circuit court involved the recovery of eight hundred dollars for the purchase of a "negro boy." After a full day of deliberation, the jury found for the plaintiff. The *Wheeling Intelligencer* asserted it would likely be "the last negro sale case that will be tried in this city for several hundred years."[206]

Branding a Deserter

Marshall Marks, a member of the 11th West Virginia Infantry, had been home on leave during the Jones-Imboden Raid. Claiming his parents induced him to desert, Marks joined the Confederate ranks. He was captured later by Union troops and jailed for desertion at the

Wheeling Athenaeum. There, on December 21, he was branded with the letter "D" on the left hip. Reportedly, Marks "barely" flinched as the hot branding iron scorched his skin.[207]

Averell's Salem Raid

A December raid by Union Gen. William Averell and 2,500 mounted men was a masterpiece of deception. Duping Confederate generals Fitzhugh Lee, Jubal Early, John Imboden and others, Averell's raiders rode the length of the new state, bound for the Virginia and Tennessee Railroad at Salem, Virginia. There the raiders tore up tracks, burned depots, storehouses, water tanks and a railroad turntable—severing a lifeline to Confederates in the western theater. Dodging thousands of veteran enemy troops, Averell's men backtracked through driving rains, flooded rivers and bitter cold, reaching Beverly in time to celebrate Christmas dinner.[208]

1864—Bushwackers and Land Pirates

Summary of Events:

Free blacks and former slaves join the Union army to fight for liberty.

The breakdown of civil law emboldens thieves, bounty jumpers and counterfeiters.

County seats are reduced to rubble.

"Bogus" government officials are arrested and jailed.

Disloyal preachers, printers, soldiers and citizens are censored or tossed into the penitentiary.

Guerrillas and "Home Guards" trade atrocities—orders of "no quarter" are the rule.

"Clawhammer" Witcher's Confederate "land pirates" live up to their name.

Refugees flee to West Virginia from the burned out Shenandoah Valley, including Mennonites, "Dunkers" and other pacifists.

The election of 1864 spells trouble for an embattled President Lincoln.

Deserters leave the Confederate army in droves.

Escape from the Athenaeum

Kate Brown and Sarah Coonrod were imprisoned at the Athenaeum in Wheeling on charges of "cutting telegraph wires and giving aid and comfort" to the Confederates. After several months of imprisonment, they managed to break the lock on the prison door. Reaching a hallway, they were met by a soldier accomplice of the 19th Pennsylvania Cavalry, who furnished them with uniform coats and caps. Thus attired, they passed the guards and escaped. Oddly, the two women returned a night later to surrender.[209]

Rendezvous for Freedom

A company of "negro soldiers" garnered attention as they arrived in Wheeling. These new volunteers were on their way to a general rendezvous of Union troops at New Brighton, Pennsylvania. The *Daily Intelligencer* remarked that they were "a fine able bodied squad," ready to give fits to the Rebels.[210]

A Lady in the Ranks

In January, several Confederate prisoners were placed in the guardhouse at Harpers Ferry. One of those inmates was later determined to be a woman! The "gay young Miss" was given an outfit of lady's clothing and released. She was later spotted on the streets of Harpers Ferry, a teenager of "prepossessing appearance,"—the "belle of the town." It was ascertained that she lived nearby, and had secretly followed her lover into the Confederate army. So well disguised was she that her lover did not recognize her for some time at company drill. He persuaded her to go home, but the "love sick girl" returned and was captured by the Yankees. She refused to take the oath of allegiance, determined to join him again.[211]

A Desperate Rebel Robber

Confederates under Hurston Spurlock of the 8th Virginia Cavalry captured the deputy sheriff of Cabell County, the commissioner of revenue, a magistrate and several Union soldiers. Spurlock's Rebels stole more than five hundred dollars—part of a regular practice of theft from county seats. Members of the Third West Virginia Cavalry pursued and routed the Rebels near Wayne Court House. They caught Capt. Spurlock, "one of the most desperate men in the country, brave, determined and uncompromising." He was wearing the hat taken from a Union officer he had killed on Big Sandy River.[212]

The Purloined Paddleboat

On February 2, the Government steamer *B. C. Levi* paddled upstream from Point Pleasant toward Charleston with Gen. Eliakim Scammon, his staff, and forty Union soldiers aboard. Halting for the night at Red House, the steamer was boarded at daybreak by Confederate raiders who demanded unconditional surrender. Scammon gave up without a fight. The Rebels paroled and released their captives, set fire to the steamer, mounted Gen. Scammon on a "miserable" old horse and made off with thousands of dollars in plunder.[213]

Judge Thompson's Trials

George W. Thompson, a circuit judge, former U. S. Attorney and Congressman, had butted heads with Gov. Pierpont over the constitutionality of West Virginia. Although his sons were in the Confederate army, the judge was a vocal opponent of secession. Removed from office and jailed three times for "treasonous" intensions, he refused to take a loyalty oath and was directed to leave the state. Using his influence, the judge had Gov. Pierpont arrested as he traveled through Ohio! Judge Thompson finally took the oath, but maintained he was a "strict constructionist" and "not a secessionist."[214]

Strange Railroad Heist

A band of Confederates under Maj. Harry Gilmor halted a passenger train near Kearneysville. Discovering a safe, they looked in vain for the key. The safe was examined "wistfully," but it was too heavy to crack or carry off. Instead, the Rebels robbed the passengers of money, watches and other valuables, working with the speed of "experienced highwaymen." It was alleged to be the first time during the war that a train had been captured for no military purpose.[215]

Stupid Drunk?

A talented attorney in civilian life, Col. George Latham of the 2nd West Virginia (mounted) Infantry, represented himself valiantly during a court-martial trial. The case arose from personal animus by his superior, the West Point-trained Gen. William Averell. Ably defending himself and his men from the charges, Latham countered that Averell had been "drunk, staggering drunk, vomiting drunk, stupid drunk" when issuing an order in question during the Battle of White Sulphur Springs![216]

A War-torn Town

The West Virginia legislature debated whether to move the Pocahontas County seat. Senator Samuel Young of Pocahontas maintained that Huntersville, the current seat of government, was "situated in a wilderness." There were "only five or six houses in the place," and not another habitation "for miles in any direction." Huntersville, claimed Young, was a "drunken, dirty town" ravaged by war, a "rallying hole of treason." Armies had burned the courthouse and other buildings. The only living thing Young saw on his last visit was "a half starved cat."[217]

Southern Stowaways

Two Confederate soldiers were captured on March 1st in Marion County. They had been in hiding at the home of Alpheus Hood—concealed between the ceiling and weatherboarding of his dwelling. Hood was arrested for sheltering the pair and all three were jailed in Wheeling.[218]

Political Prisoners

Gen. John Imboden's Confederates captured two members of the "bogus" West Virginia legislature: Senator Aaron Bechtol and Delegate Joseph Wheat, along with Morgan County Prosecutor Robert Finn and another Unionist in Bath (Berkeley Springs). Imprisoned at the notorious "Castle Thunder" in Richmond, Del. Wheat informed other inmates that he would not remain long, as "he had left a Governor at home who was not in the habit of permitting his people to be stolen." Black merchants who frequented the prison kept Wheat abreast of developments in his case. "A sharper set of fellows [I] never saw," declared Wheat. Fulfilling his boast, Wheat and the others were soon released.[219]

A Thick-Skinned Scout

Nine Confederate scouts robbed a store in Tucker County and were pursued up Dry Fork River by Capt. Nathaniel Lambert's Home Guards. Coming upon the sleeping Rebels at the "Sinks," Lambert's men opened fire, killing two. While pulling the boots off Lorenzo Adams, they saw signs of life. Clubbing Adams in the head with a gun, they left him for dead. Adams regained consciousness, but lost his balance and fell into the campfire, badly burning his hands. Although reportedly shot eighteen times, he survived the ordeal![220]

Traitorous Preachers

A meeting of the Union citizens of Marion County adopted resolutions protesting that certain clerics of Hessville had dared to "proclaim their treason from the pulpit." These preachers contrived to support the rebellion by "denouncing our Government and rulers as a usurpation, and the war we are waging to maintain Liberty and Union as unconstitutional." The Unionists urged trustees of the various churches to close their doors to such "underhanded treason."[221]

Dinner and an Abolition Speech

In late March, the citizens of Moundsville held a splendid dinner for furloughed soldiers of the 4th and 7th West Virginia Infantry regiments. A speech by R. C. Holliday, a prominent member of the Marshall

County bar, opened the "gay and festive" event. More than a thousand soldiers and civilians looked on as Holliday spoke. He opined that "the cause of the war was slavery," and demanded that the conflict be prosecuted until "the last rebel in arms" surrendered. He urged the Federal Constitution be amended "to prohibit slavery from every foot of its soil," and that the people should reelect that "honest patriot," President Abraham Lincoln. Amid cheers and spirited applause, soldiers marched into a dining room and attacked the "groaning tables" of food.[222]

A Counterfeit Caper

Private James Robinett of the 1st West Virginia Infantry received an offer to buy counterfeit "greenbacks" at a discounted price. Reporting this to his superiors, Robinett was detailed to complete the transaction under supervision of U.S. Marshals. Arrests were made, and many "counterfeit fives" from the Western Reserve Bank of Ohio were discovered. Private Robinett had uncovered a "large gang of the scoundrels" operating in several states.[223]

Bounty Jumper

Hiram Morris enlisted in the 15th West Virginia Infantry at Independence, Preston County, and collected a $65 bounty. A surgeon had rejected him for "rheumatism" in an earlier attempt. A few days after enlistment, Morris deserted and joined a different company to collect another bounty. The examining surgeon, Dr. Hazlett, had rejected Morris earlier, and happened to remember him by a deformed finger. Morris was promptly arrested for "bounty jumping."[224]

Comely Mail Carrier

Sallie Pollack, a seventeen year-old resident of Cumberland, Maryland, was arrested and charged as a Confederate mail carrier. She had been carrying letters and packages to and from Rebel sympathizers since age fourteen. Tried and convicted by a military court, she seemed to be "well posted" on troop movements in West Virginia, and had letters addressed to Robert E. Lee and Jefferson Davis when nabbed. A member of the 6th West Virginia Infantry escorted Sallie to Wheeling, preparatory to her imprisonment in Pittsburgh for the duration of war.[225]

Give Me Back My Bullets

A raid by McNeill's Rangers and affiliated Confederates on the B&O Railroad facility at Piedmont proved embarrassing to the enemy. The raiders burned extensive railroad workshops and machinery, wrecked engines, and derailed a passenger train containing more than fifty Union soldiers. The Yankees, members of the Veteran Reserve Corps, were powerless to resist—they had arms, but no ammunition![226]

Letter to the Jailer

Van Cicero Amos was lodged in jail at Morgantown, charged with stealing horses. In the wee hours of May 6, a band of Confederates dashed upon the jail and freed him. Amos left a letter in his cell for the jailer: "To-night I leave you. I would stay and see my trial through with, but the Union party are using all influence against me … I only ask for a fair trial, but on account of my politics, they won't give me justice; therefore, I shall tarry with them no longer … Prison is not for the innocent. VAN C. AMOS"[227]

Nabbed by a Newfoundland

A huge Newfoundland dog, abandoned at the Union House in Wheeling, spent most of his days asleep. But the colossal canine was roused by the pursuit of a prisoner, and joined in the chase. The dog overtook the fleeing felon, seized him by the boot, and squatted in the mud. The prisoner kicked free, but the dog caught him again, hanging on until Union authorities came up and captured him. It was suggested that the Provost Marshal present the shaggy hero with "a brass collar."[228]

Pranking a Rebel

Two young women of Paw Paw, Morgan County, schemed to have a little fun. Disguising themselves in Union army outfits, they took up arms, mounted horses, and rode to the home of an elderly friend, a well-known secessionist. Rousting him from bed at gunpoint, they forced the old fellow to a tree outside where they dangled a noose and pretended to hang him. The poor man begged for his life until the masquerading women revealed themselves. The frightened fellow could not see the humor in their prank![229]

A Troubled Marriage

A young married man joined the Union Army and marched off to war. He was killed in action at Perryville, Kentucky, and buried on the battlefield. The sad news of his death was delivered to his wife. Determined to recover his remains, she was assisted by kind friends who brought back his coffin and reburied it in the family cemetery. The young widow mourned his demise for over a year before remarrying. Months later, an exchanged prisoner passed through town with a message from her "dead" husband. He was a Rebel prisoner, alive and well, expecting to be released any day![230]

Dan Dusky's Rifle

Union forces found the rifle of an infamous guerrilla named Dan Dusky. Like its owner, the gun was a true curiosity, a long-distance killing machine. The rifle weighed no less than fifteen pounds, had a bore "five eights of an inch in diameter," and carried a ball weighing "at least one ounce." Half stocked, "heavily rifled" and massively mounted with brass, it contained a heavy load when confiscated, no doubt intended to send some Union soldier to his grave.[231]

The Rebels are Coming!

Two horsemen dashed into Morgantown crying out "the rebels are coming!" The news spread "like wildfire" that a body of Confederates had breached the B&O Railroad between Grafton and Fairmont, captured a great many horses and destroyed government property. The militia was called out; all was "bustle and confusion." It turned out that a small band of thieves had stolen horses from some citizens at Haymond's Church near Grafton, while the owners were attending worship services.[232]

Deserted over a Witch

Billy Basham, a member of the Flat Top Copperheads, deserted his Confederate comrades on account of disturbing letters from home. It seemed that Basham's wife had trouble with a witch! The witch cast various spells over Basham's family: cows refused to give milk, stones hurled from the sky, and pigs ran in circles until they dropped dead. Basham moved his family to Wyoming County to steer clear of the sorceress.[233]

Washington Moves to Wheeling

During Gen. David Hunter's Lynchburg campaign, Union forces pushed south through the Shenandoah Valley, burning barns, mills and government buildings, including the Virginia Military Institute at Lexington. A bronze statue of George Washington stood "naked and unprotected" after the conflagration at VMI. Col. David Strother, a celebrated artist and Hunter's chief of staff, saw to it that the statue was shipped to Wheeling—removed from "a disloyal people to the loyal state of West Virginia, to which it properly belongs." The statue was returned after the war.[234]

Hanging the "Greenbrier Martyr"

David Creigh, a pious and respected Greenbrier County magistrate, caught a Union soldier abusing his family. Creigh and the intruder locked in a fierce struggle, tumbled down a staircase, and ended with the soldier's death. Fearing that Union authorities would not give him a fair trial, Creigh and friends hid the body in an abandoned well. Months later, a tip led to recovery of the remains, and a drumhead court-martial found David Creigh guilty of murder. On June 11, following a forced march, Creigh received his sentence. Allowed to write a final letter home, he was hanged for the crime of defending his family. A Richmond newspaper called this incident "one of the darkest and most horrible tragedies of the war."[235]

A Soldier Censored

A correspondent of the 12th West Virginia Infantry at Gauley Bridge, writing of Union Gen. Hunter's defeat at Lynchburg, listed only the casualties suffered by his regiment: "In the conduct of this retreat I am not at liberty as a member of the army to speak my sentiments, being forbidden by the articles of war from either praising or blaming my superior officers. I therefore say nothing at all as the truth may not be told."[236]

Death by Swamp Dragon

Bernard Dolan, a member of McNeill's Rangers, was killed in a skirmish with Union "Swamp Dragons" near Petersburg. Dolan had formerly been a store clerk at Wheeling. He had signed up with the Confederate "Shriver Grays" in 1861, but deserted to join McNeill's band. According to the *Wheeling Intelligencer*: "Of the one hundred deluded young men who left this city to join their fortunes with the rebellion, not more than ten are now in the army."[237]

Printers in the Penitentiary

On July 9, Union Gen. David Hunter ordered the post commander to arrest Lewis Baker and O. S. Long, editors and proprietors of the *Wheeling Daily Register*. Their office and printing plant were seized to suppress publication of the newspaper. Baker and Long were to be jailed "until further orders." The mandate was prompted by the "general disloyalty of the sheet."[238]

Thankful for Freedom

Some fifty black refugees returned from Lynchburg with Gen. Hunter's command. After bathing in the Ohio River at Wheeling, the men proposed to enlist in the Union army. The citizens of Wheeling were touched by their great joy and animation at a prayer meeting—thankful to be rid of slavery and the Rebels![239]

A Black Confederate

Raids led by Union Gens. Crook and Averell added a steady stream of new inmates to the Athenaeum in Wheeling. Among the Rebel prisoners was a "negro soldier." He wore a "regular rebel uniform" and claimed he was trying to get through the lines when he was captured and impressed into Confederate service. The "Johnnies" insisted he was one of their own.[240]

Memorial to Mulligan

The citizens of New Creek (Keyser) met to pay tribute to Col. James A. Mulligan of the 23rd Illinois Regiment, recently killed in battle near Winchester. They mourned the loss of the heroic Irishman, "a devoted patriot, a gallant officer" a "true soldier of the Republic" and a "warm friend" who had protected the people of Hampshire and adjacent counties. Tendering their sympathy to Mulligan's "bereaved and disconsolate" widow, the grateful citizens pledged to cherish his memory.[241]

Boreman's Bounty

President Lincoln's call for 500,000 new recruits authorized West Virginia to raise one new regiment and fill others that had been depleted. To meet the state's quota, Governor Boreman proposed lucrative bounties: $100 for a one-year enlistment, $200 for two years, and $300 for three years. The governor urged potential recruits to sign up and "AVOID THE DRAFT." He warned that drafted men would not be able to avoid service by paying a commutation fee, for "men, not money, must fill the demand."[242]

Thieving Guerrillas

More than forty armed guerrillas stormed into Newark, Wirt County, on August 19 to pilfer and plunder. Targeting the stores of Unionists, they stole dry goods, boots and "notions" pointed out by sympathetic citizens. From the post office, they made off with some eight hundred postage stamps, letters and all the paper (a scarce commodity) they could carry. Valuable horses were seized and loaded with large sacks of guerrilla plunder. A citizen they sought had witnessed the sordid affair while he cowered in a cornfield, swearing vengeance![243]

A "Colored" Regiment

During the summer of 1864, runaway slaves and freedmen flocked to the Union lines in West Virginia. Many enlisted in the army as "United States Colored Troops." More than two hundred joined the 45th USCT, the lone regiment of black soldiers accredited to the state. They signed up in towns such as Wheeling, Grafton, and Clarksburg and trained at Camp William Penn in Philadelphia, under the direction of white officers. The regimental flag, designed by a black artist, portrayed a black soldier grasping "Old Glory," standing proudly beside a bust of George Washington. The 45th USCT faced discrimination in camp, but won laurels on the battlefield.[244]

A Slave-Trading Unionist

John Gilliland of Greenbrier County was a farmer and "negro and horse trader" whose opposition to secession led to his imprisonment by Confederate authorities. Released eight months later, Gilliland went on to serve as a delegate in the West Virginia legislature. While visiting his family in Greenbrier County, he was shot and killed by an unknown assailant. Gilliland's role as a slave trader *and* a fierce foe of the Confederacy highlights the strange divisions in West Virginia.[245]

Bucked and Gagged for Davis

John Kelley, a resident of Wheeling, was arrested and committed to the Athenaeum for "hurrahing for Jeff Davis." He denied the charge at first, but when confronted with the lie became "very violent." Kelley called the officers and soldiers "damned abolitionists," swearing he could "whip the whole gang of them." So disorderly and offensive was Kelley that he had to be "bucked and gagged."[246]

Dodging the Draft

In federal court, Simon Woodruff was charged with attempting to evade the draft. Woodruff sought an exemption, claiming to be over 45 years of age. As evidence, he presented a family bible in which his birth had been recorded. The court determined that a recent change had been made to the year of birth—the figure "9" had been altered to an "8," making it appear that Woodruff was born in 1818, rather than 1819. When confronted with this fact, Woodruff denied the charge. Further pressed, he admitted that his wife might have made the change, and finally, that he had done it himself![247]

A Vote for Lincoln

A meeting of the Union Campaign Club in Wheeling urged loyal citizens not to be complacent about getting out the vote in November—it was crucial for the "preservation of the Union." Several candidates for the legislature came forward with campaign speeches, and pledged support for President Abraham Lincoln. Gibson Cranmer claimed the fact that Lincoln had "signed the bill admitting West Virginia to the Union" was reason enough to reelect the embattled President.[248]

Heartless Home Guards

Dr. William Park, a citizen living near Ravenswood, Jackson County, had his horse impressed by "Capt. Kennedy's (Union) Home Guards." Park requested the privilege of riding to town with the Unionists, to see if he could get the horse released. As the party moved out, one of the Home Guards shot Park in the head, killing him instantly. The poor doctor's only transgression had been to vote for the Virginia ordinance of secession in 1861.[249]

Clawhammer's "Land Pirates"

In late September, Confederate raiders under Lt. Col. Vincent "Clawhammer" Witcher rampaged through the heart of West Virginia in search of horses, cattle and plunder. The raiders seized more than $5,000 from the Exchange Bank at Weston, robbing stores and civilians with equal delight. A soldier stopped Dr. Thomas Camden at gunpoint and demanded his watch, a family heirloom. Another Rebel accosted Camden and took his penknife. Camden also lost his horse and a fine pair of boots. However, the Rebel who stole his boots handed them back with the remark, "they are a little small."[250]

Surrounded by Secessionists

A mass meeting of Unionists was held in Martinsburg on October 1 in preparation for the upcoming elections. Although surrounded by secessionists and daily threats of Rebel raids, these Berkeley County Unionists swore allegiance to the "Government of West Virginia" and resolved to preserve the Union, the Constitution and "the laws of the land." They heartily endorsed President Lincoln and strongly approved of "the Emancipation Proclamation … and the arming of persons formerly held in slavery, as wise and efficient war measures."[251]

Racist Rants and a "Pole Raising"

As elections neared, patriotic demonstrations became plentiful across the new state. Distinguished speakers addressed the "McClellan club" in Wheeling, as supporters of Democratic presidential nominee Gen. George McClellan listened to calls to "save the Union as it was"—without the abolition of slavery. An audience filled with "Copperheads" listened to racist rants as well. To combat the McClellan supporters on October 10, Unionists of South Wheeling raised a "magnificent Lincoln and Johnson pole." Their "gay pennant" waved prominently from a wooden flagpole more than 170 feet above the ground![252]

A Glorious Greeting

A torchlight parade and rally for the Lincoln and Johnson ticket in Wheeling on October 14 was called "the greatest political demonstration ever held in the city." Hundreds of houses and public buildings glowed with "Union lights." Bands played martial music as thousands gathered to hear speeches by Senator Waitman Willey and other luminaries. While the festivities were in progress, a regiment of United States Colored Troops approached the city by steamboat. Dazzled by the illuminations, the flares and fireworks, those soldiers thought the demonstration was in their honor and could hardly be "kept aboard the boat."[253]

Dunkers on the Run

While Union Gen. Phil Sheridan waged "total war" in the Shenandoah Valley, forlorn refugees streamed into West Virginia. Among the displaced were Mennonites, "Dunkers," and other pacifists who refused to join the armies and were persecuted for their religious beliefs. Several hundred families of religious objectors crossed the Allegheny Mountains, many bound for a new life in Ohio. Their descendants remain there to this day.[254]

A Tragic Muster Out

A train collision on the B&O Railroad west of Mannington on October 24 killed or seriously injured more than a dozen members of Company F, 6th West Virginia Infantry. Of the twenty-one soldiers of the company on board, only one escaped without injury. In addition to the loss of life, the accident was rendered more tragic by the fact that these hardy Civil War veterans had just been mustered out of service.[255]

The Battle of "Stones and Bats"

A pre-dawn raid on Union forces at Beverly, Randolph County, proved costly to Capt. Hannibal Hill's 360 Confederates. Expecting to catch the enemy asleep, they charged into town with a fierce "Rebel Yell"—

only to find 200 members of Lt. Col. Robert Youart's 8th Ohio Cavalry in the ranks for roll call. Youart's troopers rushed to their huts for weapons, rallied and then countercharged to rout the Rebels with great loss. The feat was more remarkable in that Youart's force was armed with the "Union" carbine, condemned by the Ordnance Department as a "worthless weapon." Some of Youart's men fought only with "stones and bats."[256]

Murdered for McClellan

A robbery by guerrillas in Burton, Wetzel County, heightened tensions in the neighborhood. When citizens gathered to express indignation at the raid and discuss the upcoming election, Isaac Morford expressed his sentiments by "hurrahing for McClellan and Pendleton," candidates on the Democratic ticket running against President Lincoln. A Union soldier took umbrage at the taunts, had words with Morford and shot him dead![257]

"Copperheads" in Our Midst

President Lincoln won reelection in 1864 with a 68% majority in West Virginia. However, his margin of victory was slim or nil in a number of counties bordering the Ohio River. Most surprising of all was the vote in Ohio County, home of the Unionist stronghold of Wheeling, where Lincoln barely outpolled George McClellan. Remarkably, conservative Unionists or "Copperheads" felt free to cast their vote *viva voce* (by voice) despite the presence of Union bayonets.[258]

Christmas Came Early

Confederate cavalry under Gen. Tom Rosser surprised the Union defenders of New Creek Station (Keyser) on November 28, bagging a large number of soldiers and civilians, along with several hundred head of cattle, horses and a multitude of plundered goods. Many of the prisoners escaped, as the Rebels were "stone blind drunk" from captured commissary whiskey. Among the escapees was a civilian who had left a package containing $8,000 with a woman for safekeeping.

Upon returning to New Creek, he could not find the woman—or his money!²⁵⁹

Harking Back to "the Burning"

A reporter for the *New York Post* described the scene around Martinsburg. He noted the sad plight of hundreds of refugees huddled around campfires, and interviewed veteran soldiers fresh from Union Gen. Phil Sheridan's recent campaign. A group of soldiers recalled their orders to "burn out" the Shenandoah Valley. "Well," said one, "I tell you, 'tis pretty hard … The Captain, he picks his men" (here they all grinned) … "and then we get orders to burn every barn, every stack of grain, everything except the houses, and then we start the people … you see the most 'em's secesh families; the women are Union—to a man," he winked, "and their husbands, and brothers, and sons are in with the rebs; but for all that it's hard when the women come out on their knees crying and praying, and the children clinging to 'em."²⁶⁰

Renouncing the Rebellion

News of Lincoln's reelection sparked rumors that the Richmond government would soon draft enslaved people and freedmen into the Confederate army. The big question, as one writer proposed, was: "Will the negroes fight for the South?" Based on the growing number of desertions by Confederate soldiers and the many free and enslaved blacks fleeing to West Virginia, the answer seemed obvious.²⁶¹

A Cold-Hearted Killing

Guerrillas entered the Harrison County home of Henry Swiger on the night of December 16 and roused him from sleep. With faces blackened to hide their identities, the outlaws demanded money. Swiger offered a few dollars from his pockets. Demanding more, the bandits followed Swiger through a doorway and opened fire as he retrieved some "greenbacks"—murdering him in the presence of his wife. This was one of many outrages in the area. The villains were believed to be local men, deserters from both armies. One was caught and killed nearby, with black stains still visible on his face.²⁶²

No Quarter for Guerrillas!

Maj. Gen. George Crook, commanding the Department of West Virginia, issued a directive deploring the countless acts of theft, murder and other outrages by guerrillas. Crook urged the citizens to "organize for home protection, hunt and kill in any manner you please these rebel thieves." He demanded that "no quarter" should be given, and pledged to support their acts. Echoing the general in a December 23 address, West Virginia Governor Arthur Boreman bemoaned the gangs of guerrillas who "infested the state … stealing, robbing and murdering," even killing and abusing "defenseless women and children." The governor called on citizens to capture or kill these "banditti," executing "summary justice" when appropriate.[263]

Forsaken Refugees

A group of refugees stopped in the town of Beverly to share sad tales of their dreadful journey from the Shenandoah Valley. Threats of conscription into Confederate service drove them from their Rockbridge County homes. Near the turnpike on Greenbrier River, the group encountered Rebel guerrillas, "armed to the teeth." The cutthroats opened fire, killing and wounding several of the unarmed travelers. The panicked survivors fled into the wilderness. Guided only by a pocket compass, they scrambled through laurel thickets on Cheat Mountain and wandered for days near starvation before reaching civilization.[264]

Deserters in Despair

As 1864 closed, Confederate soldiers deserted in droves. In some cases they surrendered to Union authorities, swore an oath of allegiance, and moved to Ohio or other northern states. Their forlorn appearance often sparked mirth. A typical pair, shoddily clothed and shivering in the cold, were likened to a "stage version of the apothecary in Romeo and Juliet," and his accomplice, a gaunt, starved chap who "might have been mistaken for his shadow."[265]

1865—From Ruin to Restoration

Summary of Events:

Confederate Gen. Tom Rosser pulls off a daring winter raid at Beverly.

The West Virginia legislature abolishes slavery.

McNeill's Rangers grab two Union generals from under the nose of thousands.

Guerrillas continue to reap a fearsome toll.

Lawlessness and despair permeate the Mountain State.

Defeat stalks the Confederacy as war winds to a close.

Lee's surrender sparks wild celebrations, but the news of President Lincoln's assassination casts gloom over the land.

The return of "walking skeletons" highlights the deplorable conditions in prison camps.

Former soldiers come home, mostly in peace.

Rosser's Raid on Beverly

Confederate Gen. Tom Rosser, desperate to supply his suffering command in the Shenandoah Valley, launched a daring winter raid on the Union depot at Beverly. Braving bitter cold, ice and deep snow, 300 of Rosser's Rebels struck the town before dawn on January 11. Almost a thousand Union soldiers were roused from their beds after a late-night dance. The Confederates captured nearly 800 bluecoats, along with a treasure trove of supplies and civilian plunder. The liberal consumption of "John Barleycorn" allowed many to escape, but some 600 Union prisoners were marched barefoot through the snow to Virginia.[266]

Burning Stalnaker's Rails

Following their successful raid at Beverly, Rosser's Confederates camped on the farm of Hamilton Stalnaker, a few miles south of Huttonsville. Snow covered the ground—the night was bitterly cold. Shivering soldiers dismantled Stalnaker's rail fences and lit blazing fires to warm themselves. No rails were touched on the adjoining farm of Stalnaker's brother Warwick. Seeing this, Hamilton Stalnaker complained to Rosser. "General Rosser," said he, "I am one of the strongest southern men in all this country and you have burnt all my rails; while brother Warwick is one of the strongest northern men in all this country, and you have not touched his rails." Rosser looked at him and said: "Never mind, Mr. Stalnaker; we will get to Warwick's rails after awhile."[267]

Romancing the Rebels

Gen. Tom Rosser's renown as a Rebel raider followed him after the war. At a party in Baltimore, Rosser met a former Union soldier who chuckled upon hearing his name. When Rosser asked what was so amusing, the Yankee pulled him aside. "Did you lead a raid on Beverly in 1865," he inquired. Rosser nodded in the affirmative. "You took breakfast with Mrs. ____, that morning, didn't you?" "Yes," Rosser replied, but he couldn't place this man. "Well, didn't you go upstairs with her daughter, Miss _____, and didn't you make desperate love to her?" Rosser was dumbfounded: "I did, but how in thunder do you know all about it?" "Oh, you see," smiled the soldier, "I was hiding under the bed!"[268]

Removed for Disloyalty

The West Virginia legislature voted to remove Judge John W. Kennedy of the Tenth Judicial Circuit for "disloyalty." Testimony was given that the judge had ridden through the streets of Harpers Ferry, waving his hand and yelling "Huzza! Old Abe Lincoln has run away from Washington City—Huzza!" Further, Kennedy had appointed a "rebel" as sheriff of Jefferson County, and a former Confederate soldier as sheriff of Berkeley County as well. Fueling the outrage, Judge Kennedy had called the West Virginia government a "bogus concern," and he had moved to Maryland![269]

Slavery Abolished!

West Virginia's founders had dodged the slavery question in 1862. As written, the Emancipation Proclamation applied only to the Confederate states, but pressure from Congress resulted in a clause added to the West Virginia constitution calling for the *gradual* emancipation of enslaved people. By 1865, the tide of public opinion had changed. On February 3, the West Virginia legislature passed a measure that would have been almost unthinkable two years earlier: "All persons held in service or labor as slaves in this state are hereby declared free."[270]

Reclaiming Cabell?

Delegate James Ferguson, known as the "Father of Wyoming County," gave an alarming report to the West Virginia legislature on February 13. As stated by Ferguson, "a party of about two hundred rebels, formerly belonging to the commands of Gens. Jenkins and Witcher," had returned to Cabell County and had "elected a clerk and organized a government under the rebel authority."[271]

Capture of Generals Kelley and Crook

A daring raid by some sixty members of McNeill's Rangers in the early morning hours of February 21 netted two high-ranking Union generals. Lt. Jesse McNeill's Confederates rode through ice and snow in Union army overcoats, captured all the picket guards, and entered Cumberland, Maryland, without firing a shot. Hand picked Rebels quietly entered two hotels, roused Maj. Gen. Ben Kelley and Maj. Gen. George Crook from sleep, and withdrew with their prisoners on fresh horses—under the nose of several thousand Union soldiers. This exploit was called "one of the most thrilling" of the war. Gen. Crook later married the sister of one of McNeill's men![272]

A Reluctant Recruit

President Lincoln's latest call for recruits offered bounties and other inducements to avoid the draft. A Wheeling man with marital problems headed for the Provost Marshal's office to sign up. Waylaid by his wife and children, the man ignored her appeals, but as "the little ones climbed up his legs and tugged at his coat tails," he melted and followed them home. A recruiting officer thought the woman "ought to be arrested for discouraging enlistments."[273]

Seeking a Substitute

Counties that failed to meet their quota of Union volunteers were forced to institute the draft. Some able-bodied men avoided conscription by hiring a substitute. With the end of war in sight, the hiring of substitutes was brisk business. Men of means who were unwilling to join the ranks paid handsome sums for another to take their place. In this lucrative trade, with bounties and other premiums, it could pay more to enlist as a private than to accept an officer's commission.[274]

Walking Skeletons

The release of Union soldiers from Confederate prisons brought their suffering to light as the men traveled north. A correspondent wrote that many of the prisoners passing through Wheeling looked like "walking skeletons," and could move about "only with the assistance of a heavy staff or crutches." Lt. Jacob Core of the 6th West Virginia Cavalry claimed he had witnessed the deaths of "thousands of our soldiers from starvation and want of care" in Southern prisons.[275]

Rats were Scarce

Newt Bosworth of Beverly suffered as a prisoner of war in Union hands at Point Lookout, Maryland. "I will never believe that the prisoners at Andersonville or any where in the South were treated as we were," he recalled. Rations were meager and the inmates poorly clothed. They were cold and starving "all the time." One day Bosworth passed the tent of two comrades who were eating fried rats. "They smelled mighty good," he recalled, "but I was not invited to partake." Bosworth quizzed one of them later and was told there could be no sharing, as "rats were too scarce."[276]

Pistol Packing Mama

Guerrilla raiders broke into a home in Ceredo, Wayne County, and murdered Jack Meadows (Middaugh)—shot him through the heart. His wife and children were driven outside as the outlaws set fire to the premises. Seizing a revolver, Mrs. Meadows killed one guerrilla and badly wounded another, until one of them broke her leg with a rifle butt. Startled by her courage, the marauders fled. The fire consumed the house and all contents. Now widowed and homeless, the dauntless Anna Meadows moved her family to Kentucky.[277]

Stoking the Flames

Lightning raids by Rosser, McNeill, and other Confederates stoked fear in Union hearts. Citizens trembled at the thought of "bold dashes" by Rebel rangers and guerrillas as spring approached. Conspiracies to burn major northern cities added to the angst. Despite the "waning fortunes of the Confederacy," an influx of "strange faces" in many West

Virginia towns brought rumors of plots to burn out the inhabitants. As one sage warned: "A desperate enemy is a dangerous enemy."[278]

Celebrating Lee's Surrender

On the evening of April 7, word reached Clarksburg that Robert E. Lee's Confederate army had surrendered to Gen. Grant—the war was over! The city was "illuminated" in short order. Carlin's Battery Band played patriotic airs; dignitaries addressed a crowd swelling with excitement. But soon the news arrived that all was premature—Lee had "not quite" given up. Lee's surrender took place two days later, on April 9, in the village of Appomattox Court House, Virginia. The next evening, a "glorious" celebration began anew in Clarksburg. Once again, the city was a brilliant "blaze of light," with bonfires, music, a two hundred-gun salute from Carlin's Battery, and, of course, more political speeches.[279]

Lamenting Lincoln's Death

The assassination of Abraham Lincoln by John Wilkes Booth stunned America. A grand jury in Hancock County Circuit Court passed resolutions on April 18 expressing "sorrow over the said calamity which has befallen us … [L]ast week this nation was rejoicing over the glorious victories which had crowned our brave soldiers … Today the land is covered in mourning and filled with lamentations over the murder of our President at the moment he was holding out the olive branch … In this hour we would counsel forbearance and … we would remember that vengeance belongeth to the Lord."[280]

Rejecting Former Rebels

In the weeks following Lee's surrender, the citizens of some West Virginia counties passed resolutions forbidding the return of former Rebels. Many asserted that those who had left their homes to join the Confederate army should not "be permitted to return and live among us." In a May 5 letter to the U.S. Secretary of War, West Virginia Governor Arthur Boreman echoed their beliefs about the former Rebels.[281]

Rules for Rebels

General Orders of May 5-6, issued by the Department of West Virginia, directed that Confederate soldiers surrendering to military authorities would be "granted the same terms as those given to General Lee's Army." Confederate deserters and refugees could sign an oath of allegiance and return home, unless it was "dangerous to the community for them to remain." Guerrillas were to be treated as "banditti," subject to imprisonment if taken alive.[282]

The Long Walk Home

James Hall served the Confederacy from the first fight at Philippi all the way to Appomattox. Hall's 31st Virginia Infantry, more than 850 strong in 1861, numbered less than sixty men at the time of their surrender. Hall jotted in his war diary on April 12: "We marched out within the Yankee lines this morning and 'stacked our arms.' Saw several acquaintances in the Yankee army. Some of our neighbors." Released on parole, Hall "marched" most of the way home to Barbour County, a distance of more than two hundred miles. Reaching home more than two weeks later, the last entry in his diary reads: "Went fishing."[283]

Harding's Last Shot

Confederate Capt. French Harding fired his last shot at Union forces almost ten days after Lee's surrender. Harding learned of Lee's capitulation from captured letters, but refused to believe it. On May 23, he approached a squad of Union cavalry near Huttonsville. Armed with three pistols, he scribbled his parole on a scrap of paper and rode forward to turn himself in. Insulted by Sheriff Jesse Phares—the man he had shot during the Jones-Imboden Raid two years earlier—Harding drew one of his pistols, but cooler heads prevailed. The two men later became friends. Phares summoned Harding as a witness to his defense in a postwar lawsuit over tax receipts, and in his effort to secure a pension as compensation for the wound.[284]

State of the State

In a May 26 "Address to the People" of West Virginia, Governor Arthur Boreman bemoaned the "ruin, devastation and death," the lack of "civil authority," and the dearth of commerce in much of the state. Boreman hoped to withdraw U.S. forces "at the earliest possible moment," but the presence of guerrillas and other "outlaws" still threatened the peace. The governor noted that some parts of the state remained disloyal and pledged swift punishment for anyone inciting violence. Judges, sheriffs and prosecuting attorneys would be appointed until elections could be held. The governor closed with hope for West Virginia: "Let us, then, not only restore peace to her borders, but place her on the high road to prosperity."[285]

Francis H. Pierpont, *the "Father of West Virginia," never served as governor of the state.* (Author's collection)

An Odd Conclusion!

The return to peace came slowly in West Virginia. Although often unwelcome, many former Confederates returned home and became good citizens. But partisan violence continued to break out, and U.S. soldiers were sometimes called to keep the peace. Sadly, former slaves found their new liberty to be tenuous.

Wary of their conquered foe, West Virginia Republicans punished the former Confederates. The legislature restricted rights of citizenship with "test oaths." Former Confederates could not vote or hold office; nor could they practice law, teach school, sit on juries or petition the courts. In some counties, a majority of the voters were disenfranchised. Passage of the 15th Amendment to the U.S. Constitution in 1870 gave blacks the right to vote; it also fueled a push to "let up" on old enemies in gray.

As a result, former Confederates joined conservative Unionists to give Democrats a sweep of the 1870 state elections. Most rights of citizenship were restored. West Virginians framed a new state constitution, in a convention led by Samuel Price, the former Lt. Governor of *Confederate* Virginia. Ratified in 1872, that constitution governs the state to this day. Ultimately, West Virginia was "redeemed" from the very leaders who founded the new state!

The state capitol was also in flux. First established in Wheeling, the heart of Republicanism, the capitol moved to Charleston in 1870, back to Wheeling in 1875, and back to Charleston in 1885 where it remains.

Was the creation of West Virginia a constitutional act? Virginia filed suit to reclaim Berkeley and Jefferson counties, but failed in a case that went to the U.S. Supreme Court. The court did not rule on the constitutionality of West Virginia's creation in that case, but the decision (1871) and others were considered *de facto* recognition of statehood.

West Virginia is the only successful example of secession in American history![286]

Endnotes

1. Moore, *A Banner in the Hills*, 67; Snell, *West Virginia and the Civil War*, 28-29.
2. Cometti & Summers, *The Thirty-Fifth State*, 297-298.
3. Lang, *Loyal West Virginia*, 51-52; Moore, *The Rebellion Record*, vol. 2, Rumors and Incidents, 13; Cammack, *Personal Recollections*, 15-16.
4. Lesser, *Rebels at the Gate*, 94.
5. Lowry, *The Battle of Scary Creek*, 219-220.
6. Robertson, *Stonewall Jackson*, 39, 209, 690.
7. Lesser, *Rebels at the Gate*, 41, 50.
8. Thomas, *Robert E. Lee*, 39, 209, 690; Freeman, *R. E. Lee*, IV, 382; Poole, "How Arlington National Cemetery Came to Be." *Smithsonian Magazine*, Nov. 2009.
9. Sears, *George B. McClellan*, 66-69.
10. McClellan, *McClellan's Own Story*, 47.
11. Robertson, *Stonewall Jackson*, 229.
12. *Wheeling Daily Intelligencer*, June 5, 1861; Moore, *The Rebellion Record*, vol. 1, Official Report of Col. E. Dumont, Documents, 335.
13. *War of the Rebellion, A Compilation of the Official Records* (hereafter cited as *OR*) series 1, vol. 2, 48-49.
14. Dayton, Ruth Woods. "The Beginning—Philippi, 1861." *West Virginia History*, July 1952, No. 4, 256.
15. Lesser, *Rebels at the Gate*, 61-73; Moore, *The Rebellion Record*, vol. 2, Rumors and Incidents, 82.
16. Carnes, *J. E. Hanger*, Barbour County Historical Society.
17. Moore, *The Civil War in Song and Story*, 356.
18. *The New York Herald*, June 4, 1861; Lesser, *Rebels at the Gate*, 71.
19. *Reminiscences of the Cleveland Light Artillery*, 45.
20. Lesser, *Rebels at the Gate*, 77-81.
21. *Wheeling Daily Intelligencer*, July 3, 1861; Moore, *A Banner in the Hills*, 85.
22. Moore, *The Rebellion Record*, vol. 2, Rumors and Incidents, 75.
23. *Cleveland Daily Leader*, January 21, 1861; *Wheeling Daily Intelligencer*, January 22, 23, 25, 26, 1861.
24. Leib, *Nine Months in the Quartermaster's Department*, 99-102.
25. Kepler, *History of the Three Months' and Three Years' Service of the Fourth Regiment Ohio Volunteer Infantry*, 31.
26. Beatty, *The Citizen-Soldier*, 16-17.
27. Moore, *Rebellion Record*, Vol. 3, Rumors and Incidents, 9.

28 Beatty. *The Citizen-Soldier*, 22-23.
29 Grebner, *We Were the Ninth*, 61; Gabriel, *Love and Capital*, 139-140.
30 Keifer, *Slavery and Four Years of War*, vol. 1, 194-195; Lesser, *Rebels at the Gate*, 105, 125-126.
31 Pool, *Under Canvas*, 15.
32 *Richmond Enquirer*, July 19, 1861; Moore, *Rebellion Record*, vol. 3, Rumors and Incidents, 9.
33 Frame, "David B. Hart, Rich Mountain Guide," 65-75.
34 Moore, *Rebellion Record*, vol. 3, Documents, 287.
35 McClellan, *McClellan's Own Story*, 55.
36 Howison, "History of the War," *Southern Literary Messenger*, 131.
37 *Wheeling Daily Register*, February 15, 1885.
38 Taylor, Oliver, *War Story of a Confederate Soldier Boy*, n.p. TSLA
39 Lesser, *Rebels at the Gate*, 117-118.
40 Ibid., 114-119.
41 Burnett, Alf, *Incidents of the War*, 168.
42 Moore, *Rebellion Record*, vol. 2, 291.
43 Stutler, *Newshawks of '61 Reported Campaign in West Virginia*. Stutler Collection, WVSA, 78.1.3; *Indianapolis Star*, November 21, 1928.
44 Merrill, *The Soldier of Indiana in the War for the Union*, 59.
45 Cox, *Military Reminiscences of the Civil War*, vol. 1, 64-70.
46 Lowry, *The Battle of Scary Creek*, 23, 125-126.
47 Andre, Cohen and Wintz, *Bullets & Steel*, 26; Wikipedia.org/George_S._Patton.
48 Lowry, Terry, *The Battle of Scary Creek*, 64-67.
49 Ibid., 146-148.
50 Burnett, *Incidents of the War*, 126-127.
51 Lesser, *Rebels at the Gate*, 136-137.
52 Hagy, P. S., "The Laurel Hill Retreat in 1861," *Confederate Veteran*, vol. 24, no. 4 (April 1916), 173.
53 Lesser, *Rebels at the Gate*, 138, 140, 169-170.
54 Drake, *Life of General Robert Hatton*, 375; Worsham, *One of Jackson's Foot Cavalry*, 17; R. E. Lee to his wife, September 1, 1861 in Dowdey, *The Wartime Papers of Robert E. Lee*, 68-69.
55 Pool, *Under Canvas*, 18, 45, 57.

56 John D. H. Ross to "My Dear Aunt," September 21, 1861, *West Virginia History*, vol. 45 (1984), 165.

57 Pool, *Under Canvas*, 18-19.

58 Keifer, *Slavery and Four Years of War*, vol. 1, 208.

59 [Andrews, Matthew], "Mother to the First Tennessee Regiment," *Confederate Veteran*, vol. 34, no. 8 (August 1926), 290.

60 *Cincinnati Daily Gazette*, October 30, 1861; John W. Ross to his wife, September 15, 1861, PC; Augustus Van Dyke to his father, August 29, 1861, Augustus Van Dyke Papers, IHS.

61 Bierce, Ambrose, "On a Mountain," *Ambrose Bierce's Civil War*, 7; *Wheeling Daily Intelligencer*, November 29, 1861.

62 Mills, George, *History of the 16th North Carolina Regiment*, 3.

63 Beard, Richard, "The Story of a Five-Dollar Gold Piece", *Confederate Veteran*, vol. 24, no. 2 (February 1916), 76.

64 Freeman, *R. E. Lee*, vol. 1, 577-578.

65 Watkins, Sam, "*Co. Aytch*", 16.

66 [Carrigan, Joseph C.], *Cheat Mountain*, 64, 67.

67 Taylor, *Four Years with General Lee*, 28-29; *Coldwater* (MI) *Republican*, May 24, 1878.

68 Lesser, *Rebels at the Gate*, 201.

69 *OR* vol. 51, pt. 2, 256-257; Lowry, *September Blood*, 158; *OR* vol. 5, 158-159.

70 Lowry, *September Blood*, 96-99.

71 Ibid., 127-129.

72 Lesser, *Rebels at the Gate*, 174-179, 205-212.

73 Broun, Thomas L., "Gen.. R. E. Lee's War-Horse," *Richmond Daily Dispatch*, August 10, 1886; Deitz, "Ghost of Travel[l]er, General Lee's War-Horse."

74 Taylor, *General Lee: His Campaigns in Virginia*, 31-32.

75 F. Lee, *General Lee*, 125; Freeman, *R. E. Lee*, vol. 1, 602-603; Lesser, *Rebels at the Gate*, 216-217.

76 Thomson, *Narrative of the Service of the Seventh Indiana Infantry*, 61.

77 Robert H. Milroy Papers, IHS, vol. 1, 37; Alf. Welton Diary, LC, October 21, 1861; *Wheeling Daily Intelligencer*, October 30, 1861.

78 Hull, "Some Recollections of the Civil War," *The Pocahontas Times*, March 12, 1908.

79 Cammack, John Henry, *Personal Recollections*, 39; "Cincinnati 'Times' Narrative," Frank Moore, *The Rebellion Record*, vol. 3, Documents, 165; Bierce, Ambrose, "On a Mountain," *Ambrose Bierce's Civil War*, 5-6.

80 *Richmond Daily Dispatch*, October 12, 1861.

81 James Atkins Diary, October 4, 1861, GDAH.

82 Thomson, *Narrative of the Service of the Seventh Indiana Infantry*, 56-58.

83 Victor Vallette Papers, PC.

84 Clark, Walter, *Under the Stars and Bars*, 36.

85 Geiger, Joe, Jr., "The Tragic Fate of Guyandotte," *West Virginia History*, vol. 54 (1995), 28-41; "Madie Carroll House," hmdb.org.

86 *Wheeling Daily Intelligencer*, October 25, 1861; Ben May to his brother, December 12, 1861, PC; Joseph C. Snider Diary, October 30, 1861, WVU; Hall, *Diary of a Confederate Soldier*, 35-36.

87 James Atkins Diary, transcript, November 17, 1861, GDAH; Walter A. Clark Diary, November 17, 1861, PC.

88 *Richmond Examiner*, January 7, 1862; James C. Gamble to his brother, December 20, 1861, PC; Lesser, *Rebels at the Gate*, 254, 260.

89 OR ser. 1, vol. 5, 461; Poe, *Personal Reminiscences*, 11; Thomas Prickett to Matilda, December 9, 1861, Thomas Prickett Papers, IHS.

90 Hamilton, William, *Recollections of a Cavalryman*, 25-26.

91 Bierce, "On a Mountain," *Ambrose Bierce's Civil War*, 8-9.

92 Curry, *A House Divided*, 86-88; Hall, *The Rending of Virginia*, 407, 409-410; Ambler, Atwood and Mathews, *Debates and Proceedings*, vol. 1, 438.

93 Hall, *Diary of a Confederate Soldier*, 42-43.

94 Lesser, *Rebels at the Gate*, 261-262, 268.

95 Ibid., 265-268.

96 Toney, *The Privations of a Private*, 28; Watkins, *Company Aytch*, 56-57.

97 Watkins, *Company Aytch*, 19-20.

98 Reader, *History of the Fifth West Virginia Cavalry*, 126.

99 Hermann, *Memoirs of a Veteran*, 44-46.

100 OR ser. 1, vol. 5, 405-407; Moore, *Rebellion Record*, vol. 4, 127-129.

101 Curry, *A House Divided*, 90.

102 *Wheeling Daily Intelligencer*, April 1, 1862.

103 Ibid., March 14, 1862.

104 Robert H. Milroy to Mary Milroy, April 7, 1862, JCPL; Noyalas, *"My Will is Absolute Law": A Biography of Union General Robert H. Milroy*, 36.

105 *Wheeling Daily Intelligencer*, April 28, 1862; Ibid., June 25, 1863; Egan, *The Flying, Gray-Haired Yank*, 85-87.

106 Sutherland, *A Savage Conflict*, 101; *Confederate Conscription Acts, 1862-1864*, Wikipedia.com.

107 *Richmond Daily Dispatch*, May 8, 1862.

108 *Wheeling Daily Intelligencer*, May 13, 1862.

109 OR ser. 1, vol. 51, part 2, 531-532.

110 Stutler, *West Virginia in the Civil War*, 173-177; O.R. ser. 1, vol. 12, part 1, 489-491.

111 *Wheeling Daily Intelligencer*, May 3, 1862.

112 Lowry, *22nd Virginia Infantry*, 32.

113 Armstrong, *The Battle of Lewisburg*, 127.

114 Stutler, *West Virginia in the Civil War*, 178-179; Benjamin, "Gray Forces Defeated in Battle of Lewisburg," *West Virginia History*, vol. 20, no. 1, 24-35; Armstrong, *The Battle of Lewisburg*, 215-218.

115 Benjamin, "Gray Forces Defeated in Battle of Lewisburg," *West Virginia History*, vol. 20, no. 1, 24-35.

116 *Wheeling Daily Intelligencer*, June 7, 1862.

117 Plum, *The Military Telegraph*, 104-106; Stutler, *West Virginia in the Civil War*, 43-48.

118 *Wheeling Daily Intelligencer*, July 22 and September 11, 1861; Kirkland, *The Pictorial Book of Anecdotes and Incidents of the War of the Rebellion*, 406-407.

119 Farrar, *The Twenty-Second Pennsylvania Cavalry*, 52-53; Wolfe, "General Kelley and the Rebel Girl," *Goldenseal*, (Special Fall 2013), 4-7.

120 Lesser, "Lincoln's Odd Trick: The Strange Finale to West Virginia Statehood," *Goldenseal*, (Special Fall 2013), 38-40.

121 *Wheeling Daily Intelligencer*, July 11, 1862.

122 Curry, *A House Divided*, 100-105.

123 *Wheeling Daily Intelligencer*, July 26, 1862.

124 Shaffer, *Clash of Loyalties*, 110.

125 *Gallipolis Journal*, August 14, 1862.

126 "Charges against Lt. Henry A. Myers, June 20, 1862," Ringgold Cavalry (PA), manuscript, PC.

127 *Wheeling Daily Intelligencer*, August 16, 1862.

128 Ibid., August 29, 1862.

129 Ibid., August 27, 1862.

130 Beard, "Reminiscences of Civil War Days" and Arnold, "Beverly in the Sixties," *Magazine of History and Biography*, Randolph County Historical Society, no. 13 (Elkins, WV,), 35, 71.

131 Provost Marshal's Office, Second District, W.Va., Grafton, April 17, 1865

certifying enlistment of Granville Phillips on October 18, 1864, PC; Delauter, *62nd Virginia Infantry*, 96.

132 *Wheeling Daily Intelligencer*, September 9, 1862.

133 Cheeks, "Border Rangers' Daring Raid," *America's Civil War* (January 2000), 54.

134 *Wheeling Daily Intelligencer*, September 5, 1862.

135 Robertson, *Stonewall Jackson*, 605.

136 Cobb, "Story of Moses and Margaret Phillips," *Magazine of History and Biography*, Randolph County Historical Society, no. 7 (Elkins, WV), 1933, 32-33; Plum, *The Military Telegraph*, 107.

137 *The National Tribune*, October 30, 1902; *Harper's Weekly*, November 8, 1862.

138 Lowry, *The Battle of Charleston*, 157.

139 Ibid., 183, 186-187.

140 Wintz, ed. *Civil War Memoirs of Two Rebel Sisters*, 42.

141 *Wheeling Daily Intelligencer*, October 2, 1862.

142 Ibid., October 16, 1862.

143 *OR* ser. 2, vol. 4, 640.

144 *Wheeling Daily Intelligencer*, October 28, 1862.

145 Lowry, *The Battle of Charleston*, 316.

146 *Richmond Daily Dispatch*, December 12, 1862; Maxwell, *History of Tucker County, West Virginia*, 344-345; *OR* ser. 2, vol. 5, 781, 808-811; *OR* ser. 3, vol. 3, 10-11; *Journal of the Senate of Virginia*, January 10, 1863, no. 353 in Robert H. Milroy Collection, JCPL.

147 Sutherland, *A Savage Conflict*, 162-163.

148 *Richmond Daily Dispatch*, December 12, 1862.

149 Lang, *Loyal West Virginia*, 186.

150 *OR* ser. 2, vol. 5, 121-122.

151 Lesser, "Lincoln's Odd Trick: The Strange Finale to West Virginia Statehood," *Goldenseal* (Special Fall 2013), 38-40; *Wheeling Daily* Intelligencer, January 22, 1876.

152 Keifer, *Slavery and Four Years of War*, 315-316.

153 *Wheeling Daily Intelligencer*, January 3, 7, and 14, 1863.

154 Shaffer, *Clash of Loyalties*, 92-96; *Wheeling Daily Intelligencer*, January 17 and 24, 1863.

155 *OR* ser. 2, vol. 5, 155; *Richmond Daily Dispatch*, September 2, 1862.

156 *Wheeling Daily Intelligencer*, January 3, 1863.

157   *OR* ser. 1, vol. 21, 1093-1094; *Richmond Daily Dispatch*, January 16, 1863.

158   *Wheeling Daily Intelligencer*, February 5, 1863.

159   Curry, *A House Divided*, 10-11; *Wheeling Daily Intelligencer*, February 13, 1863.

160   *Wheeling Daily Intelligencer*, February 17, 1863.

161   Ibid., March 12 and 14, 1863.

162   *Martinsburg Weekly Gazette*, March 24, 1863.

163   Curry, *A House Divided*, 128-129.

164   *Wheeling Daily Intelligencer*, April 9, 1863.

165   Ibid., April 16, 1863.

166   Ibid., April 21, 1863.

167   *OR* ser. 1, vol. 25, part 2, 280.

168   Bond, "Storming Blockhouse in Greenland Gap," *Confederate Veteran*, vol. 17, no. 10 (October, 1909), 499.

169   Thacker, ed. *French Harding Civil War Memoirs*, 88-90.

170   *Wheeling Daily Intelligencer*, May 7, 1863.

171   *The Fairmont Times*, June 8, 1934; Collins, *The Jones-Imboden Raid*, 117-120.

172   *OR* ser. 1, vol. 25, part 1, 120; *The Rockingham Register*, June 6, 1863; Collins, *The Jones-Imboden Raid*, 164-167.

173   Camden, *My Recollections and Experiences of the Civil War*, 49-56.

174   www.historynet.com/sergeant-milton-humphreys-concept-of-indirect-fire.htm.

175   *Wheeling Daily Intelligencer*, May 11 and June 6, 1863; Moore, *A Banner in the Hills*, 206; Rice and Brown, *West Virginia: A History*, 152.

176   *Wheeling Daily Intelligencer*, June 9, 1863.

177   Ibid., June 20 and June 22, 1863.

178   Ibid., April 14, 1863.

179   Arnold, "Beverly Under Artillery Fire," *Confederate Veteran*, vol. 36, no. 1 (January 1928), 14-15.

180   *Wheeling Daily Intelligencer*, June 10, 1863; *Journal of the Senate of the State of West Virginia*, Wheeling: John F. McDermot, Public Printer, 1863.

181   *Wheeling Daily Intelligencer*, July 15, 1863.

182   *OR* ser. 1, vol. 27, part 2, 943-945, 1000-1005.

183   *Wheeling Daily Intelligencer*, July 18, 1863.

184   Ibid., July 22, 1863.

185   Ibid., July 24 and July 25, 1863.

186 Ibid., August 10, 1863.

187 Ibid., August 11, 1863.

188 Ibid., August 13, 1863.

189 *Staunton Spectator*, September 8, 1863; *Wheeling Daily Intelligencer*, September 9, 1863; Wittenberg, *The Battle of White Sulphur Springs*, 137, 165n.

190 *OR* ser. 1, vol. 29, part 1, 38; Wittenberg, *The Battle of White Sulphur Springs*, 96.

191 Patton, *The Pattons: A Personal History of an American Family*, 48.

192 Wittenberg, *The Battle of White Sulphur Springs*, 45-46, 118, 132-133.

193 *OR* ser. 1, vol. 29, part 1, 105-108; *Richmond Daily Dispatch*, September 17, 1863; *Staunton Spectator*, September 22, 1863.

194 *Wheeling Daily Intelligencer*, September 25, 1863.

195 *Wheeling Daily Register*, October 6, 1863.

196 Stutler, *West Virginia in the Civil War*, 247-252; Cook, "The Battle of Bulltown," *The West Virginia* Review, 254-256.

197 *The Weston Democrat*, April 22, 1927; Cook, "The Battle of Bulltown," *The West Virginia* Review, 254-256.

198 *Wheeling Daily Intelligencer*, October 26, 1863.

199 Moore, Frank, *Anecdotes, Poetry and Incidents of the War: North and South*, 373.

200 *Journal of the Senate of the State of West Virginia*, October 29, 1863.

201 Cook, "The Battle of Droop Mountain," *The West Virginia Review*, October 1928; *OR* ser. 1, vol. 29, part 1, 499-549.

202 James Z. McChesney to Mother, November 16, 1863, McChesney Letters, Ms78-1.1:11, WVU; Lowry, *Last Sleep: The Battle of Droop Mountain*, 148, 194.

203 Wilson, *Haunted West Virginia*, 130-132; "Ghosts of Droop Mountain," westvirginiahauntsandlegends.com.

204 *Wheeling Daily Intelligencer*, November 24, 1863.

205 *OR* ser. 1, vol. 29, part 2, 537.

206 *Wheeling Daily Intelligencer*, December 18, 1863.

207 Ibid., December 22, 1863.

208 Lang, *Loyal West Virginia*, 364-372.

209 *Wheeling Daily Intelligencer*, January 6, 1864.

210 Ibid., January 5, 1864.

211 *Wheeling Daily Register*, January 16, 1864.

212 *Wheeling Daily Intelligencer*, January 30, 1864; *OR* ser. 1, vol. 51, part 1, 211-212.

213 *The Weekly Register*, February 11, 1864; *Wheeling Daily Register*, February 15, 1864.

214 *Richmond Daily Dispatch*, January 13, 1862; *OR* ser. 2, vol. 5, part 1, 545, 548; *OR* ser. 2, vol. 6, 160-161; "Pierpont's Bastille—The Trials of Judge Thompson," *West Virginia—The Other History*, google.com.

215 *OR* ser. 1, vol. 33, 151-154; *Richmond Daily Dispatch*, February 19 and 22, 1864.

216 *Wheeling Daily Intelligencer*, February 10, 1864.

217 Ibid., February 25, 1864.

218 Ibid., March 2, 1864.

219 *OR* ser. 2, vol. 6, 1116; *Wheeling Daily Intelligencer*, July 14, 15, and 16, 1864.

220 Maxwell, *The History of Randolph County, West Virginia*, 309; Bosworth, *A History of Randolph County, West Virginia*, 155-157.

221 *Wheeling Daily Intelligencer*, April 14, 1864.

222 Ibid., March 31, 1864.

223 Ibid., April 4, 1864.

224 Ibid., May 2, 1864.

225 Ibid., May 2 and 3, 1864; *Cumberland (MD) Times-News*, August 3, 2013.

226 *Wheeling Daily Intelligencer*, May 7 and 9, 1864.

227 Ibid., May 10, 1864.

228 Ibid., May 20, 1864.

229 Ibid., May 2, 1864.

230 Ibid., May 11, 1864.

231 Ibid., May 25, 1864.

232 Ibid., June 6 and 13, 1864.

233 Summers County Historical Society, 45-48.

234 David H. Strother to Governor Arthur I. Boreman, July 8, 1864, also October 14, 1865, AR1748, box 2, folder 1, WVSA; *Wheeling Daily Intelligencer*, July 23, 1864.

235 *Richmond Daily Dispatch*, October 6, 1864; McKinney, *The Civil War in Greenbrier County, West Virginia*, 297-325.

236 *Wheeling Daily Intelligencer*, July 12, 1864.

237 Ibid., June 27 and 28, 1864.

238 Ibid., July 11 and 22, 1864.

239 Ibid., July 11, 1864.

240 Ibid., July 26, 1864.

241 Ibid., August 4, 1864.

242 Ibid., August 25, 1864.

243 Ibid., August 24 and 25, 1864.

244 Brownfield, "African American West Virginians in the Civil War," *The Carter Woodson Project*, www.marshall.edu; Peirpoint, *Annual Report of the Adjutant General of the State of West Virginia*, 1865, 369-373.

245 *Wheeling Daily Intelligencer*, August 27, 1864.

246 Ibid., September 2, 1864.

247 Ibid., September 10, 1864.

248 Ibid., September 19, 1864.

249 Ibid., September 24, 1864.

250 Camden, *My Recollections and Experiences of the Civil War*, 82-86; O.R. ser. 1, vol. 43, part 1, 639-641.

251 *Wheeling Daily Intelligencer*, October 6, 1864.

252 Ibid., October 11, 1864.

253 Ibid., October 15, 17, and 21, 1864.

254 Ibid., October 17, 1864.

255 Ibid., November 5, 1864.

256 Armstrong, *Surprise! The Confederate Raids on Randolph County, W.Va., 1864-1865*, 5-14; *Wheeling Daily Intelligencer*, November 11, 1864.

257 *Wheeling Daily Intelligencer*, November 3, 1864.

258 *The West Virginia Journal*, December 7, 1864; *Wheeling Daily Intelligencer*, November 21, 1864.

259 *Wheeling Daily Intelligencer*, November 2, 5, 6, and 7, 1864; *Richmond Daily Dispatch*, December 3, 1864.

260 *Wheeling Daily Intelligencer*, November 3, 1864.

261 *Wheeling Daily Intelligencer*, November 22, 1864.

262 *Wheeling Daily Intelligencer*, December 22 and 28, 1864.

263 *The West Virginia Journal*, December 28, 1864; *Wheeling Daily Intelligencer*, December 26, 1864.

264 *Wheeling Daily Intelligencer*, December 14, and 23, 1864.

265 Ibid., December 31, 1864.

266 Summers, ed., *A Borderland Confederate*, 86-89; *OR* ser. 1, vol. 46, part 1, 447-

449; Arnold, "Fighting in the Streets of Beverly, W. Va., *Confederate Veteran*, vol. 32, no. 4 (April 1924), 133-135; Armstrong, *Surprise! The Confederate Raids on Randolph County, W. Va., 1864-1865*, 15-34.

267 Maxwell, *The History of Randolph County, West Virginia*, 304.

268 *Highland Recorder* (VA), January 19, 1894 in Armstrong, *Surprise! The Confederate Raids on Randolph County, W. Va., 1864-1865*, 29.

269 *Acts of the Legislature of West Virginia*, Wheeling, no. 5, 1865.

270 "Chap. 10—"An Act for the Abolishment of Slavery in this State," *Acts of the Legislature of West Virginia*, Wheeling, 1865.

271 *Wheeling Daily Intelligencer*, February 14, 1865; www.wycoreport.com. "Judge James H. Ferguson known as 'Father of Wyoming County.'"

272 Maxwell and Swisher, *History of Hampshire County West Virginia*, 673-684; *Wheeling Daily Intelligencer*, February 23, 1865 and September 19, 1877; *Richmond Daily Dispatch*, February 28, 1865; Scott, "The Capture of Generals Crook and Kelley," 50-54, www.mountaindiscoveries.com, Fall 2005.

273 *Wheeling Daily Intelligencer*, February 17, 1865.

274 Ibid., March 29, 1865.

275 Ibid., March 4 and 30, 1865.

276 Reminiscence of Squire Newton Bosworth, 31st Virginia Infantry (n.d.), transcript, PC.

277 *Wheeling Daily Intelligencer*, February 21, 1865; *The Weekly Register*, March 9, 1865; Geiger, *Disorder on the Border*.

278 *The West Virginia Journal*, March 1, 1865; *Wheeling Daily Intelligencer*, March 3 and 22, 1865.

279 *The Weekly National Telegraph*, April 14, 1865.

280 *Wheeling Daily Intelligencer*, May 3, 1865.

281 Ibid., May 3 and 4, 1865; *OR* ser. 2, vol. 8, 533-534.

282 *Wheeling Daily Intelligencer*, May 10, 1865.

283 Dayton, ed., *The Diary of a Confederate Soldier: James E. Hall*, 135-139.

284 Thacker, ed., *French Harding Civil War Memoirs*, 188-203.

285 *Morgantown Weekly Post, and Monongalia and Preston County Gazette*, June 10, 1865.

286 Rice and Brown, *West Virginia: A History*, 151, 157-164; Curry, *A House Divided*, 134-135; Williams, *West Virginia: A Bicentennial History*, 86, 89-91.

BIBLIOGRAPHY

Books

Acts of the Legislature of West Virginia, at it's Third Session Commencing January 17, 1865. Wheeling, 1865.

Ambler, Charles H., Frances. H. Atwood and William B. Mathews, eds. *Debates and Proceedings of the First Constitutional Convention of West Virginia (1861-1863).* 3 vols. Huntington, WV: Gentry Brothers Printers, 1939.

Andre, Richard, Stan Cohen and Bill Wintz. *Bullets & Steel: The Fight for the Great Kanawha Valley 1861-1865.* Charleston, WV: Pictorial Histories Publishing Company, Inc., 1995.

Armstrong, Richard L. *Surprise! The Confederate Raids on Randolph County, W.Va., 1864-1865.* Privately published, 2003.

Beatty, John. *The Citizen-Soldier; or, Memoirs of a Volunteer.* Cincinnati, OH: Wilstach, Baldwin & Co. 1879.

Bierce, Ambrose. *Ambrose Bierce's Civil War.* William McCann, ed. Washington D.C.: Regnery Gateway, 1991.

Bosworth, Dr. A. S. *A History of Randolph County, West Virginia.* Elkins, WV: Privately published, 1916.

Burnett, Alf. *Incidents of the War: Humorous, Pathetic, and Descriptive.* Cincinnati, OH: Rickey & Carroll, Publishers, 1863.

Camden, Thomas Bland, M.D. *My Recollections and Experiences of the Civil War, or a Citizen of Weston During the Late Unpleasantness.* Parsons, WV: McClain Printing Co., 2000.

Cammack, John H. *Personal Recollections of Private John Henry Cammack: A Soldier of the Confederacy 1861-1865.* Huntington, WV: Paragon Ptg. & Pub. Co., 1920.

[Carrigan, Joseph C.] *Cheat Mountain; or, Unwritten Chapter of the Late War.* Nashville, TN: Albert B. Tavel, 1885.

Clark, Walter A. *Under the Stars and Bars or, Memories of Four Years Service with the Oglethorpes of Augusta, Georgia.* 1900. Reprint. Jonesboro, GA: Freedom Hill Press, Inc., 1987.

Collins, Darrell L. *The Jones-Imboden Raid: The Confederate Attempt to Destroy the Baltimore & Ohio Railroad and Retake West Virginia.* Jefferson, NC: McFarland & Co. Inc., 2007.

Cometti, Elizabeth and Festus P. Summers, eds. *The Thirty-Fifth State: A Documentary History of West Virginia.* Parsons, WV: McClain Printing Company, 1966.

Cox, Jacob D. *Military Reminiscences of the Civil War.* 2 vols. New York: Charles Scribner's Sons, 1900.

Curry, Richard O. *A House Divided: A Study of Statehood Politics and the Copperhead Movement in West Virginia.* Pittsburgh, PA: University of Pittsburgh Press, 1964.

Dayton, Ruth Woods, editor. *The Diary of a Confederate Soldier: James E. Hall.* Mrs. Elizabeth Teter Phillips, 1961.

Delauter, Roger U., Jr. *62nd Virginia Infantry.* Lynchburg, VA: H. E. Howard, Inc., 1988.

Dowdey, Clifford and Louis H. Manarin, eds. *The Wartime Papers of Robert E. Lee.* 1961. Reprint. New York: Da Capo Press, 1987.

Drake, James Vaulx. *Life of General Robert Hatton, Including his Most Important Public Speeches, Together, with much of his Washington & Army Correspondence.* 1867. Reprint. Lebanon, TN: Sons of Confederate Veterans, 1996.

Egan, Michael. *The Flying, Gray-Haired Yank; or, The Adventures of a Volunteer.* Philadelphia, PA: Hubbard Brothers, 1888. Reprint. Gauley Mount Press, n.d.

Farrar, Samuel Clarke. *The Twenty-Second Pennsylvania Cavalry and the Ringgold Battalion, 1861-1865.* Akron, OH and Pittsburgh, PA: The New Werner Company, 1911.

Freeman, Douglas S. *R. E. Lee: A Biography.* 4 vols. New York: Charles Scribner's Sons, 1934-1935.

Gabriel, Mary. *Love and Capital: Karl and Jenny Marx and the Birth of a Revolution.* New York: Little, Brown and Company, 2011.

Geiger, Joe Jr. *Disorder on the Border: Civil Warfare in Cabell and Wayne Counties, West Virginia, 1856-1870.* 35th Star Publishing, 2000.

Grebner, Constantine. *"We Were the Ninth": A History of the Ninth Regiment, Ohio Volunteer Infantry April 17, 1861 to June 7, 1864.* 1907. Reprint translated and edited by Frederick Trautmann. Kent, OH: The Kent State University Press, 1987.

Hall, James E. *The Diary of a Confederate Soldier.* Ruth Woods Dayton, ed. Privately published, 1961.

Hamilton, William Douglas. *Recollections of a Cavalryman of the Civil War after Fifty Years, 1861-1865.* Columbus, OH: The F. J. Heer Printing Co., 1915.

Hermann, Isaac. *Memoirs of a Veteran*. 1911. Reprint. Lakemont, GA: CSA Press, 1974.

Howison, Robert R. "History of the War." *Southern Literary Messenger*. Vol. 37 (March 1863).

Journal of the Senate of the State of West Virginia. Wheeling: John F. McDermot, Public Printer, 1863.

Keifer, J. Warren. *Slavery and Four Years of War*. 2 vols. New York: G. P. Putnam's Sons, 1900.

Kepler, William. *History of the Three Months' and Three Years' Service of the Fourth Regiment Ohio Volunteer Infantry in the War for the Union*. 1886. Reprint. Huntington, WV: Blue Acorn Press, 1992.

Kirkland, Frazer. *The Pictorial Book of Anecdotes and Incidents of the War of the Rebellion*. Hartford, CT: Hartford Publishing Company, 1867.

Lang, Theodore F. *Loyal West Virginia From 1861 to 1865*. Baltimore, MD: The Deutsch Publishing Co., 1895.

Lee, Fitzhugh. *General Lee*. The Great Commanders Series. New York: D. Appleton and Company, 1894.

Leib, Charles. *Nine Months in the Quartermaster's Department; or The Chances for Making a Million*. Cincinnati, OH: Moore, Wilstach, Keys & Co., Printers, 1862.

Lesser, W. Hunter. *Rebels at the Gate: Lee and McClellan on the Front Line of a Nation Divided*. Naperville, IL: Sourcebooks, Inc., 2004.

Lowry, Terry. *22nd Virginia Infantry*. Lynchburg, VA: H. E. Howard, Inc., 1988.

_____. *September Blood: The Battle of Carnifex Ferry*. Charleston, WV: Pictorial Histories Publishing Company, 1988.

_____. *Last Sleep: The Battle of Droop Mountain*. Charleston, WV: Pictorial Histories Publishing Co., 1996.

_____. *The Battle of Scary Creek: Military Operations in the Kanawha Valley, April-July 1861*. Revised Edition. Charleston, WV: Quarrier Press, 1998.

_____. *The Battle of Charleston and the 1862 Kanawha Valley Campaign*. Charleston, WV: 35th Star Publishing, 2016.

Maxwell, Hu. *The History of Randolph County, West Virginia*. Morgantown, WV: The Acme Publishing Co., 1898. Reprint, McClain Printing Co., 1961.

_____. *History of Tucker County, West Virginia.* Kingwood, WV: Preston Publishing Company, 1884. Reprint. McClain Printing Company, 1971.

Maxwell, Hu and H. L. Swisher. *History of Hampshire County, West Virginia.* Morgantown, WV: A. Brown Boughner, Printer, 1897.

McClellan, George B. *McClellan's Own Story.* William C. Prime, ed. New York: Charles L. Webster & Company, 1887.

McKinney, Tim. *The Civil War in Greenbrier County, West Virginia.* Charleston, WV: Quarrier Press, 2004.

Merrill, Catherine. *The Soldier of Indiana in the War for the Union.* Indianapolis, IN: Merrill and Company, 1864.

Mills, George Henry. *History of the Sixteenth North Carolina Infantry Regiment in the Civil War.* Hamilton NY: Edmonston Publishing, Inc., 1992.

Moore, Frank, ed. *The Rebellion Record: A Diary of American Events.* 12 vols. New York: G.P. Putnam, 1861-1868.

_____. *Anecdotes, Poetry and Incidents of the War: North and South. 1860-1865.* New York: Printed for the Subscribers, 1866.

_____. *The Civil War in Song and Story.* New York: P. F. Collier, 1889.

Moore, George E. *A Banner in the Hills: West Virginia's Statehood.* New York: Appleton-Century-Crofts, 1963.

Noyalas, Jonathan A. *"My Will is Absolute Law:" A Biography of Union General Robert H. Milroy.* Jefferson, NC: McFarland & Company, Inc., 2006.

Patton, Robert H. *The Pattons: A Personal History of an American Family.* New York: Crown Publishers, 1994.

Peirpoint, Francis P. *Annual Report of the Adjutant General of the State of West Virginia for the Year Ending December 31, 1865.* Wheeling, WV: John Frew, Public Printer, 1866.

Plum, William R. *The Military Telegraph During the Civil War in the United States.* 2 vols. Chicago: Jansen, McClurg & Company, 1882.

Poe, David. *Personal Reminiscences of the Civil War.* Buckhannon, WV: Upshur-Republican Print, 1911.

Pool, J. T. *Under Canvas; or, Recollections of the Fall and Summer Campaign of the 14th Regiment Indiana Volunteers, Col. Nathan Kimball, in Western Virginia, in 1861.* Terre Haute, IN: Oliver Bartlett, 1862.

Reader, Frank S. *History of the Fifth West Virginia Cavalry, Formerly the Second Virginia Infantry, and of Battery G, First West Va. Light Artillery.* New Brighton, PA: Daily News, 1890.

Reminiscences of the Cleveland Light Artillery. Cleveland, OH: Cleveland Printing Company, 1906.

Rice, Otis K. and Stephen W. Brown. *West Virginia: A History.* The University Press of Kentucky, Second Edition, 1993.

Robertson, James I. *Stonewall Jackson: The Man, The Soldier, The Legend.* New York: Macmillan Publishing, 1997.

Shaffer, John W. *Clash of Loyalties: A Border County in the Civil War.* Morgantown, WV: West Virginia University Press, 2003.

Snell, Mark A. *West Virginia and the Civil War: Mountaineers are Always Free.* Charleston, SC: The History Press, 2011.

Stutler, Boyd B. *West Virginia in the Civil War.* Charleston, WV: Education Foundation, Inc., 1963.

Summers County Historical Society. *The Civil War in Summers County, West Virginia.* Charleston, WV: Quarrier Press, 2021.

Summers, Festus P., ed. *A Borderland Confederate.* Pittsburgh, PA: University of Pittsburgh Press, 1962.

Sutherland, Daniel E. *A Savage Conflict: The Decisive Role of Guerrillas in the American Civil War.* Chapel Hill, NC: The University of North Carolina Press, 2009.

Taylor, Walter H. *Four Years with General Lee.* New York: D. Appleton and Company, 1878.

_____. *General Lee: His Campaigns in Virginia, 1861-1865, with Personal Reminiscences.* 1906. Reprint. Lincoln, NE: University of Nebraska Press, 1994.

Thacker, Victor L., ed. *French Harding Civil War Memoirs.* Parsons, WV: McClain Printing Co., 2000.

Thomas, Emery. *Robert E. Lee: A Biography.* New York: W. W. Norton & Company, 1995.

Thomson, Orville. *Narrative of the Service of the Seventh Indiana Infantry in the War for the Union.* n.d. Reprint. Baltimore MD: Butternut and Blue, 1993.

Toney, Marcus B. *The Privations of a Private.* Nashville, TN: Privately published, 1905.

Watkins, Sam R. *"Company Aytch:" Maury Grays First Tennessee Regiment or, A Side Show of the Big Show.* 1882. Reprint. Ruth H. F. McAllister, ed. Franklin, TN: Providence House Publishers, 2007.

Williams, John Alexander. *West Virginia: A Bicentennial History.* New York: W. W. Norton & Company, Inc., 1976.

Wilson, Patty A. *Haunted West Virginia: Ghosts & Strange Phenomena of the Mountain State.* Mechanicsburg, PA: Stackpole Books, 2007.

Wintz, William D. *Civil War Memoirs of Two Rebel Sisters.* Charleston, WV: Pictorial Histories Publishing Co., 1989.

Wittenberg, Eric J. *The Battle of White Sulphur Springs.* Charleston, SC: The History Press, 2011.

Worsham, John H. *One of Jackson's Foot Cavalry.* James I. Robertson, Jr., ed. Jackson, TN: McCowat-Mercer Press, Inc., 1964.

Periodicals

[Andrews, Matthew] "Mother to the First Tennessee Regiment." *Confederate Veteran* 34, no. 8 (August 1926)

Arnold, Thomas J. "Fighting in the Streets of Beverly, W.Va." *Confederate Veteran* 32, no. 4 (April 1924).

_____. "Beverly Under Artillery Fire." *Confederate Veteran* 36, no. 1 (January 1928).

_____. "Beverly in the Sixties." *Magazine of History and Biography.* Randolph County Historical Society, no. 13 (June 1969).

Beard, Evelyn Yeager. "Reminiscences of Civil War Days." *Magazine of History and Biography.* Randolph County Historical Society, no. 13 (June 1969).

Beard, Richard. "The Story of a Five-Dollar Gold Piece." *Confederate Veteran* 24, no. 2 (February 1916).

Benjamin, J. W. "Gray Forces Defeated in Battle of Lewisburg." *West Virginia History* 20, no. 1 (October 1958).

Bond, Frank A. "Storming Blockhouse at Greenland Gap." *Confederate Veteran* 17, no. 10 (October 1909).

Carnes, Eva Margaret. "J. E. Hanger: The First Man to be Injured by a Cannon

Ball in the Civil War and the First to Have a Limb Amputated." *The Barbour County Historical Society*, (June 3, 1961).

Cheeks, Robert C. "Border Rangers' Daring Raid." *America's Civil War*, (January 2000).

Cobb, William H. "*Story of Moses and Margaret Phillips.*" *Magazine of History and Biography*. Randolph County Historical Society, no. 7 (1933).

Cook, Roy Bird. "The Battle of Droop Mountain." *The West Virginia Review*, (October 1928).

_____. "The Battle of Bulltown." *The West Virginia Review*, (June 1933).

Dayton, Ruth Woods. "The Beginning—Philippi, 1861." *West Virginia History* 13, no. 4 (July 1952).

Deitz, Dennis. "Ghost of Traveler, General Lee's War-Horse." *Greenbrier County in the Civil War, 1861-1865*. Ronceverte, WV: Lee Headquarters Trust, Inc., 1993.

Frame, Katherine Hart. "David B. Hart, Rich Mountain Guide." *Magazine of History and Biography*. Randolph County Historical Society, no. 12 (April 1961).

Geiger, Joe, Jr. "The Tragic Fate of Guyandotte." *West Virginia History* 54 (1995).

Hagy, P. S. "The Laurel Hill Retreat in 1861." *Confederate Veteran* 24 (April 1916).

Hull, W. H. "Some Recollections of the Civil War." *The Pocahontas Times*, various dates, 1908-1909.

Lesser, W. Hunter. "Lincoln's Odd Trick: The Strange Finale to West Virginia Statehood." *Goldenseal: West Virginia Traditional Life*. (Special Fall, 2013).

Oram, Richard W., ed. "Harpers Ferry to the Fall of Richmond: Letters of Colonel John De Hart Ross, C.S.A., 1861-1865." *West Virginia History* 45 (1984).

Poole, Robert M. "How Arlington National Cemetery Came to Be." *Smithsonian Magazine*, (November 2009).

Wolfe, Richard A. "General Kelley and the Rebel Girl." *Goldenseal: West Virginia Traditional Life*. (Special Fall, 2013).

Newspapers

Cincinnati Daily Gazette

Cleveland Daily Leader

Cleveland Plain Dealer

Coldwater Republican

Cumberland Times-News

Gallipolis Journal

Harper's Weekly

Highland Recorder

Indianapolis Star

Martinsburg Weekly Gazette

Morgantown Weekly Post, and Monongahela and Preston County Gazette

Richmond Daily Dispatch

Richmond Enquirer

Richmond Examiner

Staunton Spectator

The Fairmont Times

The National Tribune

The Rockingham Register

The Weekly National Telegraph (Clarksburg, WV)

The Weekly Register (Point Pleasant, WV)

The West Virginia Journal

The Weston Democrat

Wheeling Daily Intelligencer

Wheeling Daily Register

Manuscripts

Georgia Department of Archives and History (GDAH)
James Atkins Diary, transcript

Indiana Historical Society (IHS)
Augustus Van Dyke Papers
Robert H. Milroy Papers
Thomas Prickett Papers

Jasper County Public Library (JCPL)
The Robert H. Milroy Collection

Library of Congress (LC)
Alf. Welton Diary

Personal Collection of the Author (PC)
Ben May Letters
Charges Against Lt. Henry A. Myers
Granville Phillips Papers
James C. Gamble Letter
John W. Ross Letter
Victor Vallette Papers
Walter A. Clark Diary

Tennessee State Library and Archives (TSLA)
Taylor, Oliver. "The War Story of a Confederate Soldier Boy." n.p. Extracts from the Bristol *Herald-Courier* (TN, VA), January 23-February 27, 1921.

West Virginia State Archives (WVSA)
Boyd B. Stutler Collection
West Virginia Secretary of State's Office, Miscellaneous Records

West Virginia and Regional History Collection, West Virginia University (WVU)
James Z. McChesney Letters, H. E. Matheny Collection
Joseph C. Snider Diary

Websites

Blankenship, Paul Ray. "Judge James H. Ferguson known as 'Father of Wyoming County.'" *Wyoming County Report*, September 16, 2016, www.wycoreport.com

Brownfield, Caleb. "African American West Virginians in the Civil War: The 45th USCT." The Carter Woodson Project, www.marshall.edu

"Confederate Conscription Acts, 1862-1864," wikipedia.org

Crookshanks, Ben. "Sergeant Milton Humphreys' Concept of Indirect Fire," www.historynet.com

"George S. Patton," wikipedia.org

"Ghosts of Droop Mountain Battlefield," westvirginiahauntsandlegends.com

"Madie Carroll House," hmdb.org

"Pierpont's Bastille—The Trials of Judge Thompson," *West Virginia—The Other History*, google.com

Scott, Harold L. "The Capture of Generals Crook and Kelley." Fall 2005, www.mountaindiscoveries.com

"Timeline of West Virginia: Civil War and Statehood." West Virginia Archives and History, 2021, http://129.71.204.160

Made in the USA
Middletown, DE
21 August 2022

71185256R00076